HANDS-ON
ANCIENT
PEOPLE
VOLUME I

ART ACTIVITIES ABOUT MESOPOTAMIA, EGYPT AND ISLAM

Ancient Egypt has been of interest for hundreds of years. The great civilization began 5000 years ago as a long, thin country running along the length of the Nile River. Due to the hot, dry climate and the religious practice of preserving the royal dead with treasures, we have museums full of Egyptian objects. Thirty of these artifacts have been adapted to paper and clay in an effort to replicate this remarkable culture.

This book is dedicated to Emily Mortensen my youngest daughter.
Her consulting and genuine interest in the details of a small publishing effort and her advice on management
have made a difference. Pictured is her delightful family: Spence, Anna, Lily, and Mia.

Book design by Art & International Productions, LLC, Anchorage, Alaska
Laurel Casjens took the photographs.
Mary Simpson illustrated the book and assisted with the development of the crafts.
Nancy Mathews and Madlyn Tanner edited and proofread the text.

Books by the author
from KITS Publishing:

Hands-on Africa
(ISBN 0-9643177-7-X)

Hands-on Alaska
(ISBN 0-9643177-3-7)

Hands-on American Vol. I
(ISBN 0-9643177-6-1)

Hands-on Asia
(ISBN 0-9643177-5-3)

Hands-on Celebrations
(ISBN 0-9643177-4-5)

Hands-on Rocky Mountains
(ISBN 0-9643177-2-9)

Hands-on Latin America
(ISBN 0-9643177-1-0)

Hands-on Pioneers*
(ISBN 1-57345-085-5)
*Published by Deseret Book

KITS PUBLISHING
2359 E. Bryan Avenue Salt Lake City, Utah 84108
(801) 582-2517   fax: (801) 582-2540
e-mail - info@hands-on.com web - www.hands-on.com

HANDS-ON ANCIENT PEOPLE

VOLUME I

ART ACTIVITIES ABOUT MESOPOTAMIA, EGYPT AND ISLAM

Yvonne Y. Merrill
KITS PUBLISHING

TABLE OF CONTENTS

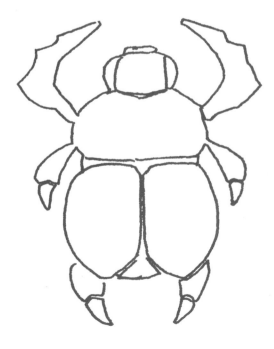

THREE CULTURES: A STUDY IN PATTERNS

Pattern is the combination of shape and color to create designs. Each of the cultures presented had sophisticated and different pattern styles. The two ancient civilizations of Mesopotamia and Egypt consistently engraved, wove, painted and wrote patterns. The Islamic and Arabic people have surpassed most with their architectural and decorative patterns, continuing today. As the activities are explored refer to the authentic pattern ideas on this page.

THE MESOPOTAMIANS

THE EGYPTIANS

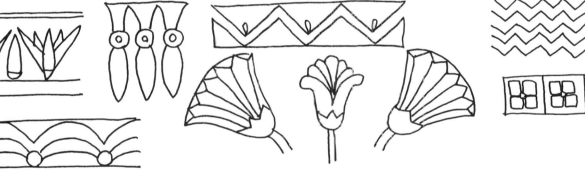

THE ISLAMIC CULTURE

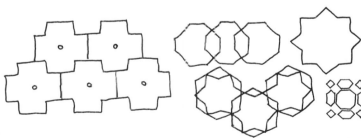

STONE-LOOKING MAGIC

Many artifacts in these arid areas are made of stone. To make stone-like projects we recommend commercial air-drying clay or this oven-baked salt clay:
2 c. flour, 1 c. salt, 1 c. water. Bake at 200-250 degrees until hard (2-4 hours).

20 FEATURED SITES ON THE MAP

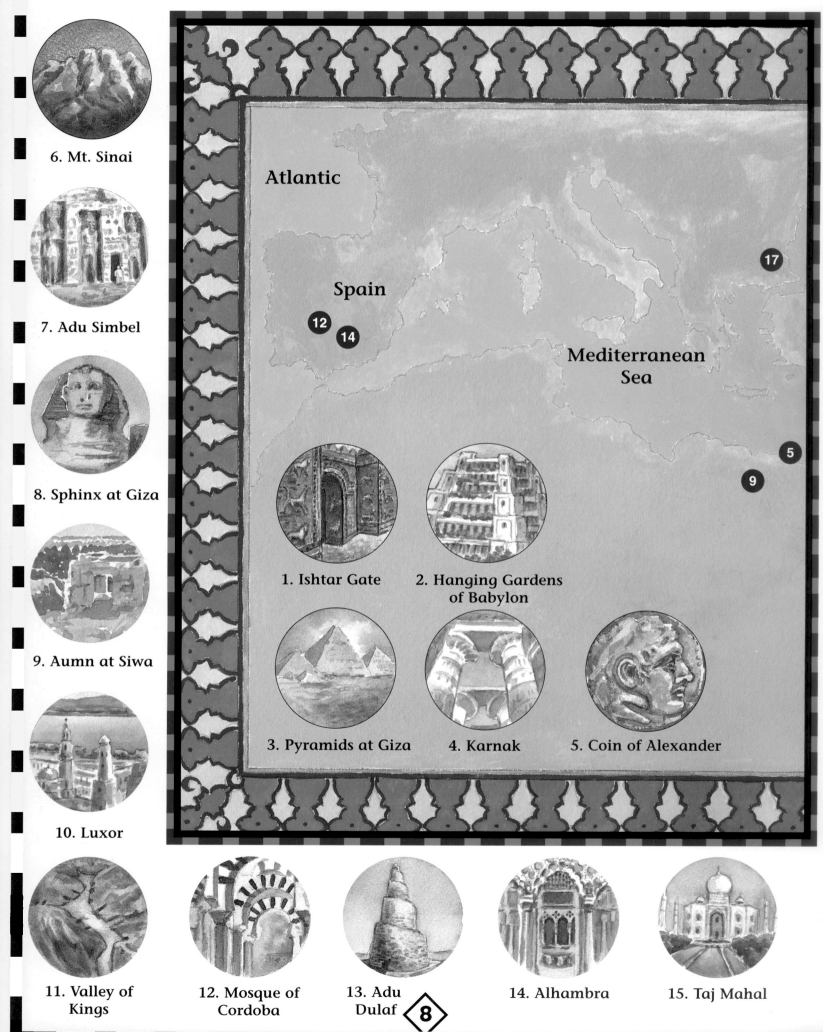

6. Mt. Sinai

7. Adu Simbel

8. Sphinx at Giza

9. Aumn at Siwa

10. Luxor

Atlantic

Spain

Mediterranean Sea

1. Ishtar Gate

2. Hanging Gardens of Babylon

3. Pyramids at Giza

4. Karnak

5. Coin of Alexander

11. Valley of Kings

12. Mosque of Cordoba

13. Adu Dulaf

14. Alhambra

15. Taj Mahal

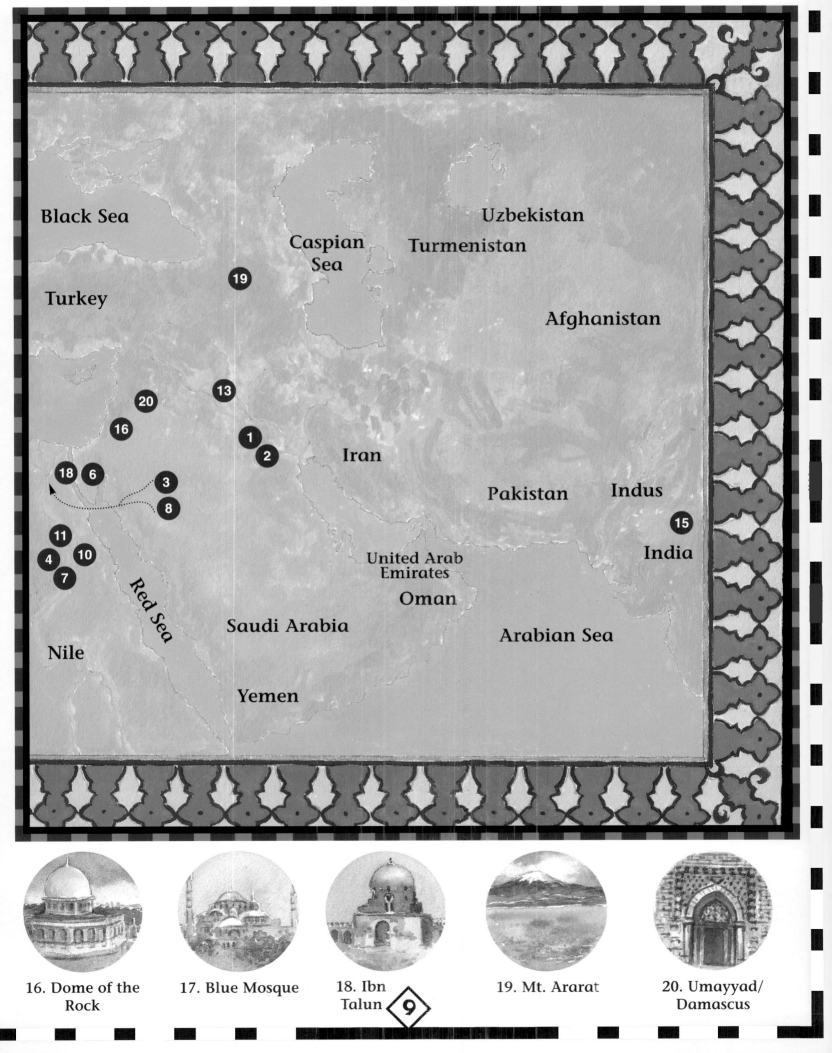

Black Sea

Caspian
Sea

Uzbekistan

Turmenistan

19

Turkey

Afghanistan

13

20

16

1

2

Iran

18 6

3

8

Pakistan

Indus

15

11

India

4   10

United Arab
Emirates

7

Oman

Red Sea

Saudi Arabia

Arabian Sea

Nile

Yemen

16. Dome of the
Rock

17. Blue Mosque

18. Ibn
Talun

19. Mt. Ararat

20. Umayyad/
Damascus

THE AMAZING MESOPOTAMIANS

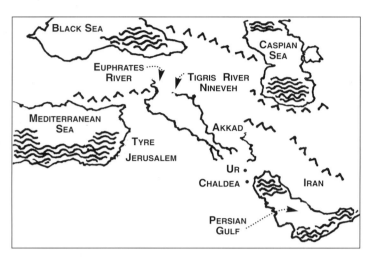

Map of ancient Mesopotamia

Map of area today

Western civilization traces its beginnings to Mesopotamia, the "cradle of civilization." Through its complex and rich history, we find evidence of the world's first experiments with agriculture and irrigation, medicine, astronomy, and architecture. Mesopotamians invented writing, used the first wheel, built the world's first cities, and developed the basic elements of modern mathematics.

A TIME LINE

10,000-3700 B.C. People lived along the Tigris/Euphrates rivers.

3700 to 2900 B.C. The oldest cuneiform tablets were found when the city of Ur was uncovered. This Sumerian city of 20,000 people was a great walled, oval-shaped site dominated by a massive temple complex called a ziggurat. In 1920 Leonard Wooley found the Royal Cemetery where several Sumerian rulers were buried in deep tombs packed with amazing goods. By 2700 B.C. the city of Ur was at its peak, and loose city-states surrounded this southern area.

2400-1750 B.C. The Akkadians invaded Sumeria and built Akkad.

1750 B.C. The date of Hammurabi's legal code, the first written laws.

1792-1595 B.C. Babylonia replaced the Akkad region and the great city of Babylon was built. The Kassites invaded and lived in Babylon. Then the Assyrians invaded northern Mesopotamia and built the cities of Nineveh and Nimrud. The Assyrians borrowed cultural strengths from others.

1400 B.C. The first Assyrian Empire. The Queen of Sheba and King of Tyre are part of this era.

820 B.C. Damascus was destroyed and the Chaldeans invaded southern Mesopotamia and restored Babylon.

586 B.C. The seige of Jerusalem when the Jews were brought by the thousands to Babylon to provide slave labor for the great buildings Sargon II wanted to build. This is known as the "exile" period.

612 B.C. The Assyrian Empire fell, and by 539 B.C. Cyrus and the Persians conquered the area.

1921 A.D. The country of Iraq was established.

CONTRIBUTIONS

WRITING can be traced to the Sumerians, the world's earliest literate and urban culture. Cuneiform tablets dating from 3300 B.C. have been found in Ur graves. (Cuneiform is a technique of pressing wedge-shaped symbols into wet clay.) Cuneiform was the writing method used by all Mesopotamians.

THE WHEEL was first invented by the Sumerians for making pottery, and archeologists speculate this wheel was eventually turned on its side and attached to a cart. Sumerian wheels did not have spokes. A famous work of art called the Standard of Ur shows the four-wheeled chariot used in war.

MEDICINE was surprisingly advanced, including drugs made from plants, animals, and minerals. Cuneiform prescriptions were used. A thorough understanding of human anatomy is evident. The skeletal remains found in Ur graves indicate surgery was practiced. Drawings categorizing plants and animals have given modern scientists clues as to what the environment was like in Mesopotamia.

CHEMISTRY of practical use interested the Mesopotamians. Colorful dyes were mixed. Fig and date wines were produced. Archeologists have discovered the world's oldest written recipe, a tablet dated 3750 B.C. recording the process for making beer.

MATHEMATICS can be traced to Sumerians in 1800 B.C. when many elements of modern mathematics were first used, including the decimal system, Arabic numbers, and the base of 60 used frequently today in 60 minutes, 360 degrees, and so on. Sumerians first used the concept of zero. Babylonians are credited with the idea of place value as well as with concepts used 1,000 years later in the Greek Pythagorean theorem.

cuneiform tablet

weights for measuring

the sun god and Ishtar

ASTRONOMY shows careful and precise record keeping which has provided valuable information about the planets, stars, and rotation of the earth. The Babylonians invented a time system based on the stars.

ARCHITECTURE shows the mastery of engineering skills, including multi-storied buildings. The varied use of stone and sand is evidence of creative construction. Glass used as glaze on pottery was invented from studying soil and sand. Bronze made from tin and copper dates back 4000 years.

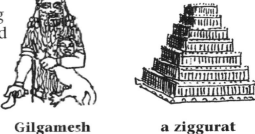

Gilgamesh   **a ziggurat**   **pottery**

MYTHS from Mesopotamia have familiar themes like Gilgamesh and the Great Flood, Pyramus and Thisbe, similar to Shakespeare's ***Midsummer Night's Dream,*** Verdi's ***Nabucco*** about the exiled Jews, and the basket of reeds and the rescuing of Moses in the Old Testament.

Babylonian Mosaics

BABYLONIAN MOSAICS FROM THE GATE OF ISHTAR

Materials: For each animal panel: 2 posterboard panels with one a few inches larger than 8 1/2" x 11", acrylic paints, brushes, sponge, glue, scissors or paper cutter, clear acrylic spray (for a shiny ceramic effect), patterns on page 80.

1. Produce a mortar-like background surface for the tiled bricks: using light grey paint, sponge-texture a large posterboard.

2. Enlarge lion or bull patterns as desired. The sample in the photograph is twice the pattern size. Glue pattern evenly onto smaller posterboard making sure all parts are securely attached.

3. Paint with acrylic paints; thin paint with water so brick patterns show through for later cutting. Let the paint dry.

4. Spray animal with clear acrylic finish. Let dry.

5. Cut painted animal along vertical and horizontal brick lines to make "tile-looking" bricks.

6. Reassemble bull or lion bricks onto faux-mortared background leaving space between the bricks for the grey mortar to show through. Glue in place.

The magnificent Ishtar Gate in Babylonia was covered with these magnificent animal mosaics. It was at the head of the Processional Way, a ceremonial street in Babylonia. It is speculated that 150,000 people of many nationalities lived in the walled city of Babylon. The ruins of Babylon were excavated in 1902 and archeologists found a building with gardens at each level. Were these the famous Hanging Gardens? The Ishtar Gate was in fine shape when it was uncovered and the animal mosaics were astonishing. The Lion, representing the goddess of Ishtar, was most often repeated. Nebuchadnezzar II built the great city in 604-502 B.C. Thousands of Israelites were brought to Babylon after the destruction of Jerusalem in 586 B.C. This story is recorded in the Bible's Old Testament.

THREE SUMERIAN CHARIOTS

THREE SUMERIAN CHARIOTS

Materials: *A piece of white or cream-colored railroad board or a manila folder 12" x 18", air-hardening clay or the salt dough recipe on page 7, a 1/8" doweling piece 20" long, fine-tipped black marker, orange and brown paint, brushes, glue, straws, 1/4" wooden dowel.*

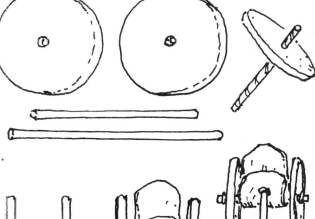

One-Person Chariot

The small one-seater chariot was probably pulled by a small animal like a dog or a goat. The museum model claims it might be 8000 years old!

1. Roll out your dough or clay and cut out two, 2" wheels. Round them with water. Cook them in a very low oven or–if clay-let them air dry overnight.

2. Cut two pieces of wooden dowel 3" and 4" long. Make axle holes with a straw. Push the short wooden piece through the holes in each wheel. You now have one of the six simple machines: the wheel and axle.

3. Mold the clay around the 2" dowel in the middle to make a seat. Insert the longer dowel at a right angle in front. Wrap extra clay around each axle dowel on the outside to keep the dowel in place. Paint the dough a wooden color when it has hardened.

Tall Back Chariot

Tall, carved, wooden-backed chariots were used by warriors and important people.

1. Cut a piece of cardboard 2" x 12" in this shape.

2. Roll out the clay or dough and cut out 2 wheels 2 1/2" wide. Make axle holes with a straw.

3. Insert a cut dowel 3" long into the prepared hardened wheels and add clay hubs. Make a glue design on the chariot cardboard. When the glue has dried, paint it brown so it resembles wood with a carved design. Lay axle over the chariot about 3" from the end. Glue.

4. Cut a 6" dowel, paint it brown, and stick it through the holes punched in the flap and the chariot back.

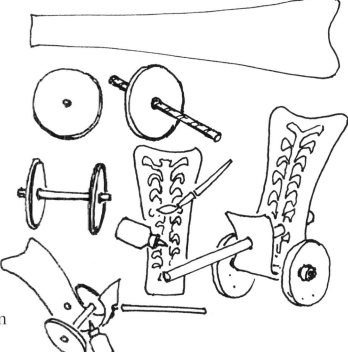

(continued on page 70)

SUMERIAN BOARD GAME

A BOARD GAME FROM SUMERIAN UR

Materials: A cardboard top or bottom of a box between 9" x 14" or larger (much smaller will not work). Twelve round discs 1 1/4" in diameter. Thick and thin black marker, a ruler, white paint, brown and orange paint, brushes and a pencil.

1. With a ruler and pencil make three long rows of eight rectangles, each one the same size. Our rectangles are 2 1/2" x 2 3/4". The rectangles will be measured according to the box size. Erase the two outside lines that make box #3 and #4. They are solid colors and NOT part of the board game (see the photograph). Draw with a strong black marker on the grid lines.

2. Paint the squares white and rub a mix of brown and orange paint on the 22 important game rectangles. (The board game was carved of ivory which becomes brownish when very old.)

3. Here are the **five** boxed patterns. Enlarge or reduce these boxes and copy them onto your game board in thick and thin black marker. Add touches of red, brown, and orange color on some squares.

4. Notice the sides of the box which are the all-seeing eye divided by various numbers of stripes.

5. Your replicated game board should be handsome and ready for the two sets of discs that are the players. Cut circles from cardboard or paper or buy wood circles. Paint 6 of one color and 6 a second color and paint five dots of black or white on each disc.

This handsome board game was excavated in the Sumerian city of Ur. It was found in a royal grave. No one has any idea of its rules or how to play it, but someone could design a fun game using their imagination from the discs and the board.

Two Ziggurats

Two Ziggurats

Materials: Any Styrofoam cone at least 10" tall and 3 1/2" at the base, a sheet of Styrofoam 2" thick by 12" x 36" long, a ruler, marker, good knife for smooth cutting, flour and paste, newspaper strips, glue, sponges for paint dabbing, brushes and paint for patterns, string, a small box.

The Cone Ziggurat

1. Wrap a piece of string around the cone and mark its spirals. These are the ramps that will be built to get to the top of the structure.
2. Mix 1 c. flour with 1/2 c. water. Mix until the paste is smooth. Add more water until it is the consistency of thick soup. The ramps are a papier-mache' process.
3. Tear newspaper strips 1"-2" wide. Make a thick base of about 15 newspaper layers and slowly build up the ramps. Make fat ramps at the bottom and thinner ramps as they approach the top.
4. Place a square on the top that could have been a temple.
5. Let the papier-mache' dry overnight. Sponge or brush paint with a clay-colored mix of orange, brown, and white.

The Stepped Ziggurat

1. Cut these Styrofoam forms:
   - a. 10" x 10" x 2" thick
   - b. 7" x 7" x 2" thick
   - c. 5" x 5" x 1 1/2" thick
   - d. 4" x 4" x 1 1/2" thick
   - e. 2" x 2" x 1" thick
2. Stack the cut pieces so they have even edges and glue them together. Let them dry for several hours with a two pound weight on top (like a book).
3. Paint any earthen-like clay color and add authentic patterns.

The best known architectural forms of Mesopotamia are the religious monuments called ziggurats or "staged towers" which dominated the important cities. Ziggurat means "the house that is the foundation between heaven and earth". The temple on the top was where the gods descended from heaven to receive offerings. Scholars suggest the form reflects mountains from a country of origin, or perhaps a giant sacrificial altar. High places have often been regarded as holy places. Ziggurats were made of clay bricks covered with limestone. They were painted with brilliant colors and patterns.

MESOPOTAMIAN PATTERNS

MESOPOTAMIAN PATTERNS

Materials: Jiffy® foam is recommended, rolls of white school art paper (24" to 36" square per person), big brushes and sponges, recycled pie tins for paint, clean-up cloths, and cardboard supports for patterns, small brushes, yardstick and pencils, scissors, white paint, paint of preferred colors, water for brushes and clean-up, pattern ideas on page 7.

1. The background paper must be prepared before you print your handsome patterns. Cut the paper the size you need (probably around a square yard or smaller). In the pie tin mix white paint, water and your background colors. **Do not stir together.** With your big sponge or brush cover the paper with uneven but blended colors. It should look old and rich in natural dye colors such as tans, yellows, soft greens, or blues.

Here are 10 sample patterns:

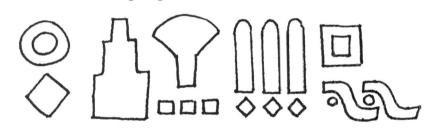

2. Sketch the design on Jiffy foam and cut it out. Mount it on a cardboard support.

3. With a pencil and yardstick lightly measure lines for the design you hope to print.

4. Put the paints for the pattern colors in individual containers. Have a small brush available for applying the paint onto the mounted design or push the design into the paint. Experiment with a scratch paper. Clean the brush with water when a new color is being used.

When the remains of Sargon II's Assyrian palace (now in Iraq) were uncovered by the Frenchman Botta in 1843, the world was astonished by the rich and superb painted patterns and mosaic work. Sir Austen Henry Layard from Britain worked in Nineveh and Nimrud writing a best-seller on his archeological finds..."especially impressive were the massive winged bulls with human heads, now in the Louvre in Paris and in New York's Metropolitan Museum of Art." Ludmilla Zemen has illustrated and retold *Gilgamesh, the King,* (1993), *The Revenge of Ishtar,* (1992), and *The Last Quest of Gilgamesh* (1995), William Heinemann Ltd., London.

MARDUK AND ISHTAR

MARDUK AND ISHTAR: BABYLONIAN GODS AND GODDESSES

Materials: Salt dough recipe on page 7, rolling pin, dull knife for cutting, a cutting surface, cereal, buttons, red hots, etc. for sticking into the dough and decorating the figure: buttons, colored cereal, candy, tools for texturing such as a nail, straw, hole of the straw, straight edge, watercolor paints, small and big brushes, foil and waxed paper, an oven, cardboard for mounting, and string or ribbon for hanging figures, patterns on pages 79 and 84.

1. For all of the figures roll a golf-ball-size dough piece out on foil with a protective piece of waxed paper. Using the pattern on page 79 cut out the dough figure. Lightly draw the body and face sections with a pencil or nail. Either texture the figure sections or decorate. When you add the decorations, brush a paste of dough and water onto the surface first; this acts as a glue.

2. Look at striding Marduk. He is textured and painted. Look at standing-tall Marduk. He is decorated, textured, and painted. Remember that the Mesopotamians loved pattern. Make a hole in the head top if you are going to hang the figure.

3. After your figure is decorated, bake it on foil for 4-6 hours in a warm oven (200 + degrees). Let the figure cool. Now it can be painted.

4. Lay the figure on a piece of cardboard and trace around it. Cut out the shape about 1/4" smaller than the tracing. Punch a hole through the cardboard that lines up with the figure hole. Generously glue the dough figure to the cardboard. Put a weight like a newspaper pile on the top. Let it dry for several hours.

5. String a ribbon or twine through the hole.

Marduk was the ruler of all Babylon's gods and the city patron deity. In the Babylonian Epic of Creation, Marduk killed troublesome monsters and also Tiamet whom he cut in half and made the sky from her top half and the earth from the bottom half. Then Marduk created humans to serve the gods. The goddess Ishtar is considered to be young, beautiful, and impulsive. She was the first goddess of fertility and love. The Greeks called her Aphrodite; the Romans named her Venus. She was the force that gave life to all: people, plants, and animals. She was the patroness of food and controlled the weather. She is often depicted with a lion whose roar represented thunder.

Christopher Moore and Christina Balit have written *Ishtar and Tammuz, a Babylonian Myth of the Seasons*, Kingfisher, NY, 1996.

CUNEIFORM

CUNEIFORM: ANCIENT CLAY MESSAGES

Materials: Air hardening clay or salt dough recipe on page 7, warm water, rolling pin, waxed paper 12" square per project, foil if baking, straws, scissors, ruler, brown, orange, yellow paint and brush or sponge, marker.

Baked Dough Message

1. Roll the dough out on foil paper with a piece of protective waxed paper on top of the dough ball. When it is 1/8" to 1/4" thick cut out a piece roughly 4" wide and 5" long. Peel away the waxed paper and the foil. Carefully place the rolled dough back on the foil for future baking.

2. Study the cuneiform wedge and curved shapes that create the Sumerian alphabet. Write down your message, translating it into cuneiform.

3. Cut a plastic straw into a "v" on one end and a curve on the other. A knife point will help to give you a clean mark.

4. Look at the clay and dough samples in the photograph. Make your message in the soft dough.

5. Oven-bake your cuneiform message on the lowest possible heat for at least 4-5 hours. Give it an ancient-looking wash with brushed-paint or a paint-dipped sponge. If the marks are hard to see, go over them with a brown small-tipped marker.

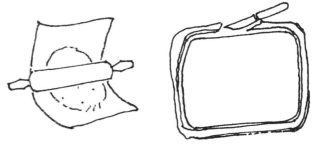

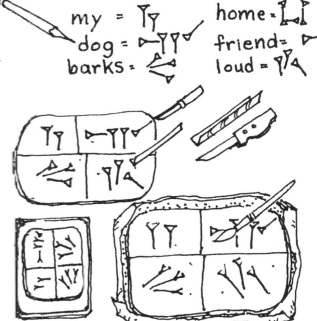

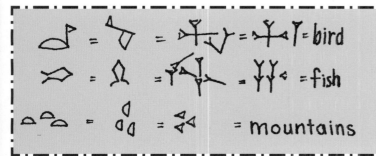

Clay Message and Envelope (like the photograph)

The clay can air dry. Proceed as with the dough project, using the same stylus (plastic straws) and knife points for the wedges.

The earliest surviving samples of writing are pictographic...simple pictures which were used to represent livestock, goods, grain sold, numbers, etc.

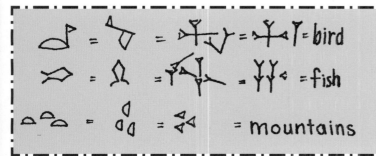

(continued on page 70)

EGYPTIAN ART AND CULTURE

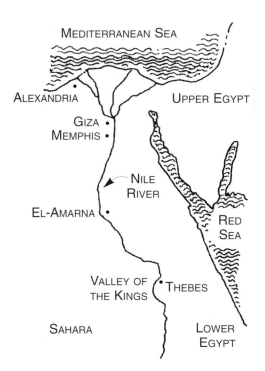

MEDITERRANEAN SEA

ALEXANDRIA

UPPER EGYPT

GIZA
MEMPHIS

NILE
RIVER

EL-AMARNA

RED
SEA

VALLEY OF
THE KINGS · THEBES

SAHARA

LOWER
EGYPT

Egypt lies on the northeastern coast of Africa, bordered by the Mediterranean Sea to the east and the Sahara Desert to the south and west. Today, Egypt's neighbors are Libya, Israel, and Sudan. In ancient times political frontiers were always changing as rival peoples like the Hittites, Assyrians, and Persians gained and lost land. Herodotus, writing in the 5th century B.C., called Egypt "the gift of the river," as without the Nile people would never have been able to survive there. They called their land "Kemet", the Black Land, because of the rich black soil in the Nile floodplain. In the south the Nile created a valley of steep cliffs and was called Lower Egypt. In the north it slowed down, spread out, and created a huge triangular area called the delta, or Upper Egypt.

GODS AND GODDESSES

Gods and goddesses hieroglyphic symbol was a flagpole sign. Flagpoles were erected at temples to remind ancient Egyptians of the invisible powers that ruled their universe. Temples were built for specific gods and employed priests. It was believed that deities used animals as temporary bodies on earth. Deities often had a male or female body and an animal's face or headpiece. Some of the most important deities as the Egyptians depicted them.

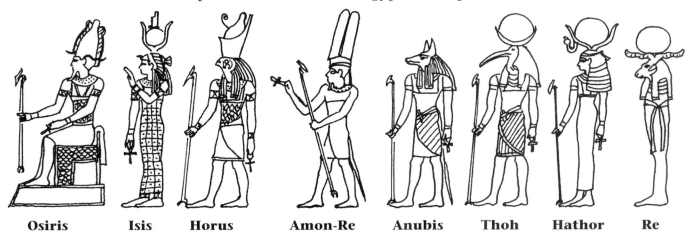

Osiris   **Isis**   **Horus**   **Amon-Re**   **Anubis**   **Thoh**   **Hathor**   **Re**

Egyptian artworks were early drawings by prehistoric hunters. Art was associated with magic. Artistic effort flourished in tombs in the form of carvings, paintings, murals, and statuary to provide the needs of the dead in the next life. Reliefs were carved on temple walls to ensure the gods could always overcome evil.

Egyptian artists were traditional and tended to copy the work of previous generations, probably because they thought there was some special power in the ancient way of showing things. Egyptians believed that pictures had great power, so they represented a scene carefully and accurately. Dangerous things were painted as harmless: for example, scorpions did not have stingers.

EGYPTIAN PERSPECTIVE

Egyptian painters had to follow strict rules about what they painted and the colors they used. They were very good at observing and portraying nature and drawing birds, animals, plants, and people.

People were shown with their head, arms hands, hips, legs, and feet as seen from the side.

Eyes, chests, and shoulders were shown from the front.

a god   a king
Gods and kings were
the largest in size.

a husband
Husbands were larger
than wives.

a wife and the children
Children were very small.

HISTORICAL BACKGROUND

Recorded history in Egypt began around 4000 B.C. when nomadic hunters settled in the Nile Valley. But it was in 3100 B.C. that Egypt crowned her first Pharoah, Menes, who later unified the country's two regions, Lower Egypt (The Delta) and Upper Egypt(from Giza to Aswan in the South). Egypt's history can be summarized as follows

Predynastic Egypt: 5000 to 3200 B.C.

Dynastic Egypt: 3200 to 2700 B.C. Development of society, law and religion

The Old Kingdom: 2700 B.C.- 2600 B.C. Great achievements especially in the fields of administration, astronomy and architecture.

The Middle Kingdom: 2260 to 1780 B.C. An era of prosperity and expansion of political strength and economic horizons. Thebes became the capital. Later, Egypt was invaded by the Hyksos, coming from Caucasia, who remained for 150 years until finally driven back.

The New Kingdom: 1580 to 1085 B.C.Four centuries of splendor, prosperity, and spiritual and artistic achievements. Architecture reaches great heights.

(continued on page 75)

SHABTI FIGURES

SHABTI FIGURES: WORKERS IN THE AFTERLIFE

Materials: Salt dough clay recipe on page 7, rolling pin, knife, foil, white, red, blue, green, black, brown, gold paint. A 10" x 10" x 3" deep box, white paper, glue, all colors of markers, an oven for baking. Note: the box is not necessary for the shabti project but they were enclosed in this type of wooden box when found in tombs, pattern ideas on page 7.

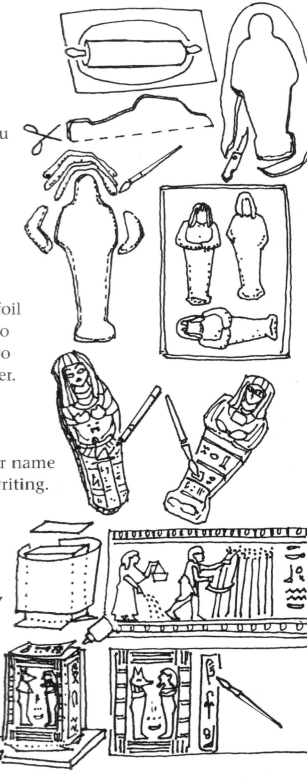

Shabti Dolls With Hieroglyphics

1. Most shabti figures were 8" long and generally the same shape. Most were painted with black hair, a whitish gown decorated with hieroglyphics and folded arms. Whichever shabti figure you make, you can paint it natural or brown, or the Egyptian blue-green of the less shapely shabti.

2. Make the salt dough. This recipe will make 6-8 figures. Roll out the dough on foil. Use a template that has been cut from a folded newspaper so it is symmetrical. Lay the template on the salt dough and cut out the doll. Carefully remove it from the foil and replace it on the foil again. Roll dough pieces to create the relief of arms, face, hair and feet. Apply to the dough by brushing on a mix of dough and water. Give the hair texture with scissors. Bake the figure in a warm oven 250 degrees for 3-4 hours.

3. Paint the figure. The hieroglyphics might be your name and a message you have made after studying this writing. (See hieroglyphics on page 47.)

Shabti Box: *Materials are any rectangular box like a small cereal box, white paper to cover the box, heavy cardboard piece for base, markers, paints, glue.*

1. Prepare your box. Measure around the box to determine the "mini mural" size. Cut the paper to fit with a piece for the top.

2. Plan the mural and border designs. The box mural shows the jackal god Anubis welcoming a shabti to the underworld. Draw and paint the mural. Glue mural to the box. Glue box flaps to the base. *(continued on page 70)*

TOYS FROM THE TOMBS

TOYS FROM THE TOMBS

Materials: Cardboard that can be cut 18" x 18", manila folder, Styrofoam balls 6" and 8" in diameter, ocher, red, black, green, brown paint, fine-tip brush, 3" square of black fabric, cotton, string and needle, red, black, beige, yellow, green markers, glue, plain paper, rubber bands, light and dark brown and orange paper, scissors, 8" of 1/4" doweling cut in half.

Ancient Egyptian Doll

1. Study the doll in the photo. Find the pattern on page 83. Copy it. Cut out the shape in heavy cardboard (for the doll base) and the same shape from a manila folder. Paint the light cardboard an earthy color and let it dry.

2. Roll the faux beads (for the hair) from brown, orange, and light brown cut strips that are 1/2" wide and 4"-5" long. Glue each end until you have about 100 paper beads.

3. Draw a pattern on the painted cardboard using the pattern ideas on page 7. Color the patterns. Glue the decorated cardboard to the heavy cardboard.

4. Cut the black fabric into a circle, stitch around the outer edge, pull the thread, and stuff the pouch with cotton. Stick it on the head knob, tightening and knotting the neck.

5. With a needle and thread string about 10 beads together and sew onto the head for hair. You should have ten lengths sewn onto the head. Dot the eyes with white-out or sew on beads for eyes.

Pull-Toy Horse

1. Find the pattern on page 83. Copy it. Cut two pieces of cardboard for the horse. Cut four 2" wheels. Make holes in the wheel centers. Paint the horse a mottled orange/yellow/brown. It is inspired by a horse toy 6,000 years old!

2. Stick the painted wood axles through each wheel. Put a piece of string through the nose for pulling the toy.

Colorful Balls

1. Cut 7-8 sections for the small ball. Color the sections with stripes, checks, and plain colors. Glue the sections onto the ball with rubber bands securing the sections while they dry.

2. Paint the larger ball sections with a stripe of gold dividing the sections.

(continued on page 71)

THE SCARAB

THE SCARAB:
AN EGYPTIAN GOOD-LUCK CHARM

The Turquoise Winged Scarab: *Materials are salt dough clay (recipe on page 7) or air drying white clay, rolling pin, foil, pattern on page 74.thread, needle, black paint, black, blue and gold markers, glue, toothpicks, paper punch, dull knife, scissors, and paper for templates.*

1. Roll out your dough/clay material to 1/4" thickness. Cut a template for the wings and beetle body on the paper fold. Place them on top of the clay piece and cut around it with the knife. Gently pick them up and place on foil or a cookie sheet. You have three pieces to dry: the middle shape for the scarab, and the dough circle as a base for the scarab, and the two wings. These can be any size as long as they are to scale. Mold the scarab onto the base with two front legs and two back legs. Make 8 holes: 2 on each wing, and 4 on the disc, and 2 on each side.
2. Bake the dough for 3-4 hours in a warm oven 200–250 degrees. Let the clay dry overnight.
3. Paint the entire piece in turquoise except the scarab. Add the black marker designs and black paint on the scarab.
4. Using black thread and a needle, sew the wings to the scarab. The piece can be mounted on gold cardboard for easier handling.

The Scarab Bracelet: *Materials are gold cardboard, salt dough, 150 rolled paper beads, cardboard closures, needle, thread, glue, paint, scissors, toothpick, gold marker.*

1. The paper beads are most effective if you paint your own paper with mottled carnelian red, lapis dark blue, and turquoise. Use gold marker on paper for the gold beads. Roll your beads. They are 1/4" thick and 3-4" long. Roll on a toothpick and glue the end.
2. Make the beetle and dry. Paint it blue. Color the 2" round cardboard disc with marker and make three holes on each side. Make the closures punching three holes in each.
3. Assemble the bracelet by stringing the beads with the needle and thread through the closures and attach to the disc holes.

(continued on page 71)

FOUR KING'S CROWNS

FOUR KING'S CROWNS

The Atef, the White Crown of Osiris: *Materials are a piece of white railroad board, all colors of paint including gold and gold marker, scissors, pattern on page 79, glue, rubber bands that are 5", stapler, paper clips.*

1. Enlarge the pattern to be 24" for back and 18" for front. Cut out the front and back. Paint the bottom edge design. **The crown head size should be 21" to 22" for an average head.** Score the crown edges 1/2" and cut notches every 2" up to the knob. Fold the notches outside the crown. Staple and glue the inside and the notches down and stand up on a tall support such as a bleach bottle or a tall vase. Carefully put big rubber bands around the crown to keep the shape as the glue dries (three or four 5" bands).

2. Cut out four pieces that are side serpents and the front cobra. Paint them. The cobra's tail is painted on the opposite side so it can go up the crown with the snake head in front.

3. Score and notch the painted side serpents. Glue them together except for the edges that will attach to the crown. Glue to the crown. Glue the cobra to the crown front. Try it on.

The Nemes, the blue "war helmet" crown: *Materials are blue railroad board, pattern on page 80 and 84, 15" x 15", gold marker, scissors, glue, stapler, paper clips, plain railroad board, patterns on pages 81,84.*

1. Cut out the five pattern pieces: two helmet sides, front and back   insets, and cobra for the front.

2. Decorate the blue helmet pieces with any type of gold disc-looking design. Glue a gold spiral snake coiling on one side. Score and notch the front and back insets. Glue and staple in place. Cut 60" of 1/2" bands from the plain railroad board. Color the bands gold with a marker. Glue the two gold side seams, and cut and glue pieces that line the helmet edge.

3. Make designs on the cobra shape with gold marker and sponge-paint white to create a contrasting color. Your helmet should be 22" around to fit an average head.

(continued on page 72)

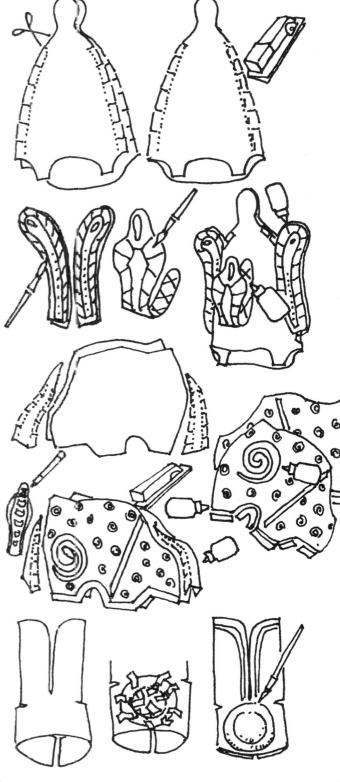

SPECTACULAR COLLARS

SPECTACULAR COLLARS

Materials: White school paper 36" x 36", ruler, pencil, scissors, glue, gold, red, green, blue markers, shiny origami paper, paper plate, 1 yard gold ribbon.

Paper Plate Collar

1. Cut out a 5" hole from the plate center. Cut a 2" gap for fitting on neck. Try the plate on the wearer and adjust the fit.
2. Pencil the design on the plate. Color the designs with fine-tipped markers.
3. Make pretty closures for the ends. Glue them on, securing the gold ties between the plate and the decorative closures.

Large Gold Collar

1. The collar is 7" wide in front and narrows to 5" wide at the back. The neck hole is 6" wide. Cut out the collar from school paper and try it on the wearer. Glue the collar onto a second paper collar for strength. It has a 1" gold edge. This step is optional.
2. Mark 1" and 2" rows with a ruler and pencil. Design each row using the four colors of Egyptian jewels: red for carnelian, blue for lapis lazuli, gold, and emerald. The actual stones in most collars were colored glass.
3. Decorate the collar with markers. Make an interesting closure to hold the gold ribbon at the back. We used a blue scarab, but many designs would be appropriate.

Shiny Gold Collar

1. This collar is 5" wide from center to the back. The neck is 7" wide. Try it on before decorating.
2. Mark 1" and 1 1/2" rows with a ruler and pencil. Go over the lines with a thick gold marker line.
3. One square of shiny origami paper for each color allows for 35 trapezoids, 70 stripes, 20 rectangles, and 20 circles. Glue pieces on with edges touching. Fix gaps with gold marker repairs. Make an interesting closure with gold such as Horus, the hawk god, and attach the gold ribbon.

The Egyptians loved to wear jewelry! Both men and women wore necklaces, bracelets, anklets, hair ornaments, earrings, pendants, and wide collars decorated with colored glass. Much of the jewelry includes images of gods and goddesses. Even pets wore jewelry. Tomb cats were painted and have been found wearing earrings and fancy collars.

EGYPTIAN DESIGNS

EGYPTIAN DESIGNS

Banner: *Materials are school paper 48" x 18", ruler, pencil, paper for templates, acrylic paints, any paint colors, brushes, black marker, 24" dowel, glue. See pattern page 7.*

1. Think about the purpose of the banner. Mark off areas that give the banner purpose. Mark all designs that are to be squares or dividers.
2. Paint the banner to look old by mixing cream paint with brown, yellow with brown, etc. Dilute the paint and apply with sponges or wide brush strokes. When it has dried, mark the design with a pencil and ruler. Paint the designs. Use a marker for hieroglyphics. If you do the symbols of ankh or a scarab, cut a template on a paper fold for symmetry. Trace around the template.
3. Fold down the paper's top edge and glue. When the glue is dry insert the dowel for display.

Frame of Matte Board: *Materials are matte board frame, ruler, pencil, black marker, paints, brush.*

1. Prepared matte frames are available at framing shops and art stores for a reasonable cost or free for educational use.
2. The same designs have been used on the frame as on the banner with a different order. After ruling and marking with a pencil, use the black marker where needed and paint the sections. Use your imagination in designing the repeated patterns.

The Terra Cotta Flower Pot: *Materials are a pot, cloth, ruler, pencil, marker, paint and brush, gold marker.*

Proceed with the pot as you did with the previous projects. Plain paper gift bags can be decorated too.

The ankh is the hieroglyphic symbol for "life". The scarab was the most important of all amulets. Thousands of scarabs of all sizes and materials have been found tucked into the linen wrappings of mummies and hung around the necks of mummies. The eye of Horus appears often in Egyptian art. The god Horus had his eye ripped out, then slit into pieces and thrown into the sea. The god Thoth found the pieces and put the eye together again. The eye form, common in art, is known as the *wedjat*. It became known as a symbol of power and healing. *Wedjats* are often found wrapped in mummy linen and placed on the mummies. Richard Balkwill has written *Clothes and Crafts in Ancient Egypt,* Gareth Stevens Publications, Milwaukee, WI, 1998.

ANIMALS, FISH AND BIRDS

ANIMALS, FISH, AND BIRDS

Glass Fish: *Materials are white school paper, scissors, pencil, 3-4 colored markets, staples or glue, stuffing, markers, brass beads, patterns on pages 82, 83.*
1. The glass fish has the same glaze pattern that the Egyptians applied to many glass containers: a wavy pattern with varying colors.
2. Cut two fish patterns on page 83 after enlarging them to the desired size. After cutting out the fish, pencil in your own wavy designs. After covering the designs with colorful markers, glue the two sides of fish together and stuff with wadding. The fish could be a hanging mobile.

The Fish Cosmetic Container: *Materials are paper, cardboard, markers, terra-cotta and green paint, brushes, scissors, a brad.*
1. Use the pattern piece on page 82, enlarging or reducing it. Cut out the bottom part by making notched lines in the cardboard and then cut with scissors. Cut out the oval center and glue on a piece of cardboard under the oval. This is a replica of a museum cosmetic container. This little bowl is where the cosmetics were placed. The vessel was carved out of wood.
2. Design the bottom section and color in with green and terra-cotta markers or paint. Cut out the top fish, paint it, and attach with a brass brad so it swings back and forth.

Canopic Jars: *Materials are a cardboard tube for each jar 4"-8" tall, glue, scissors, masking tape, blue, brown and white paint, black markers.*
1. Paint each tube a range of colors from whitish to brownish. Notch the tops about 1" and tape together into a peak. Using the patterns on page 83, cut out two paper pieces for each one. Paint them on both sides. Use your imagination. History shows us there were styles of canopic jars in every color, but the four figures never changed.
2. Glue the beaks, snouts, back, and tops of heads together. Glue the bodies onto the cardboard tubes. Paint the lines on each side with marker.

(continued on page 78)

WOMEN'S HEADWEAR

WOMEN'S HEADWEAR

Making a Paper Wig: Materials are 36" x 36" of black school paper cut into 24" x 1" strips (for the curly wig) or 1/4" strips (for the straight hair wig) attached to a paper cap, scissors, glue, stapler, a support structure for the wig (like a blender).

1. For the **straight–hair wig** cut a paper cap with 12" on each side allowed for cut hair. The cap is 10" from ear to ear and 15" from front to back (allowing 2" for cut bangs).
2. After you have cut the cap, put it on the head of the wearer and make adjustments with stapling. It should fit snugly and will take some pleating and tucking.
3. Cut the 1/4" hair strips on a paper cutter: front, back, and side. Cut the bangs with a scissors.
4. Follow the same instructions for the curly headed hair. After cutting the 1" strips, roll them around a pencil. Glue on more curly haired strips to thicken the wig.

The Gold Crowns: Materials are gold railroad board, black marker, scissors, glue, 10' of ribbon, blue, red, green and yellow paint, brushes, stapler.
The gold crown with decorative overband
1. Cut each band of gold 24" x 1 1/2" for overband crown. The overband is 15" long. Cut 6 gold discs that are 1 1/2" wide. Cut four gold eagles (or vultures) with flanges for attachment (see pattern on this page); cut a 1 1/2" rectangle for crown front.
2. Paint the decorative discs, 1 bird and front rectangle. Glue them in place.
3. Attach the overband and glue the backs together. Try on the handsome crown with one of the wigs.

The gold crown with ribbon and cobra
1. The crown band is 2" x 24". The four upright forms are 12" x 2". They are one piece and split down the middle. The cobra is 10" long. Attach the upright forms 2" apart, the middle upright piece, the 5 ribbons on the bottom edge. Staple and glue these pieces. Paint the cobra and attach tail, bending the swollen body up and head bent down.

1/2 cobra

vulture

Queens often ruled jointly with their husband kings and were called "The Great Royal Wife". One of the most powerful of queens was Nefertari. She was buried in the Valley of the Queens. Nefertiti, the chief wife of Akhenaten, had great influence over her husband. They had six daughters. The wall paintings at Amarna show the children playing with their parents. Having family intimacy portrayed was an unusual thing. Women in Egypt are painted with lighter skin because they stayed indoors. Women could own their own businesses and farms.

MUSICAL INSTRUMENTS

Musical Instruments

Hand Clappers: *Materials are plastic milk bottles or bleach bottles, strong scissors, white, yellow and brown acrylic paint, brush, a brass brad, fine-tipped black or brown marker, hand pattern page 83.*

1. Look at the plastic bottle. Find the two flattest surfaces. You must have a flat surface. Trace the hand on two flat surfaces. The hands are joined where the thumbs meet.

2. Cut out the hands at the wrist using a strong scissors or knife.

3. Paint all sides of the hands with a mix of paint. The hands were made of ivory. They are whitish to brownish. Add a second coat if needed. Let dry a few hours.

4. Pencil the decorative circles onto the top hand. Trace with a fine-tipped marker. Punch a hole at the base of each hand and push the brad parts through. Practice clapping them against your hand. How do they sound?

Sistrum Rattle: *Materials are black railroad board 12" x 12" and two strips 22" x 2", glue, scissors, strong wire, 12-15 buttons, stapler, 10" x 1/4" pencil or dowel. Pattern on page 82.*

1. Cut out the handles. The figure can look like the sample or just be a simple handle. The top must be 4"–5" wide. Glue any decorative design on the front piece and let dry. Staple the edges together. Cover up the staples with black marker. Insert a pencil or dowel piece into the handle.

2. Glue the two long bands together. Make holes with a scissor point 5" and 3" down if you want two rows of rattles. String wire with buttons through the holes. Cover wires with black tape or a paper patch.

3. Cut 1 1/2" notches 3/8" in from each side of the handle and at the end of the band. Put the slits together. Reinforce with more paper patches. Rattle your sistrum. How does it sound?

(continued on page 73)

numbers

1 = 1
tether ⌒ = 10
rope ⌒ = 100

lotus = 1,000
finger = 10,000
tadpole = 100,000

1,000,000

HIEROGLYPHICS

HIEROGLYPHICS: PICTURES AS LETTERS

***Materials:** A manila folder that has been aged with tea, coffee or dabbed brownish paint. Scissors, fine-tipped and broad-tipped black markers, pencil, eraser, a skewer, and glue, cartouche pattern on page 73.*

1. Study a hieroglyphic alphabet. Here are some of the common ones. Egyptian scribes wrote a person's name in a cartouche. You are looking at two cartouches in the photograph.

2. Age the light cardboard. Make a 1/2" border on the edge with a black marker or paint. Think about the message you wish to put on the cartouche: your name, instructions, etc.

3. Draw your message in pencil on scrap paper. Lightly draw it onto the prepared cartouche. Go over the drawn lines with a fine-tipped black marker. Ask a friend to read the cartouche.

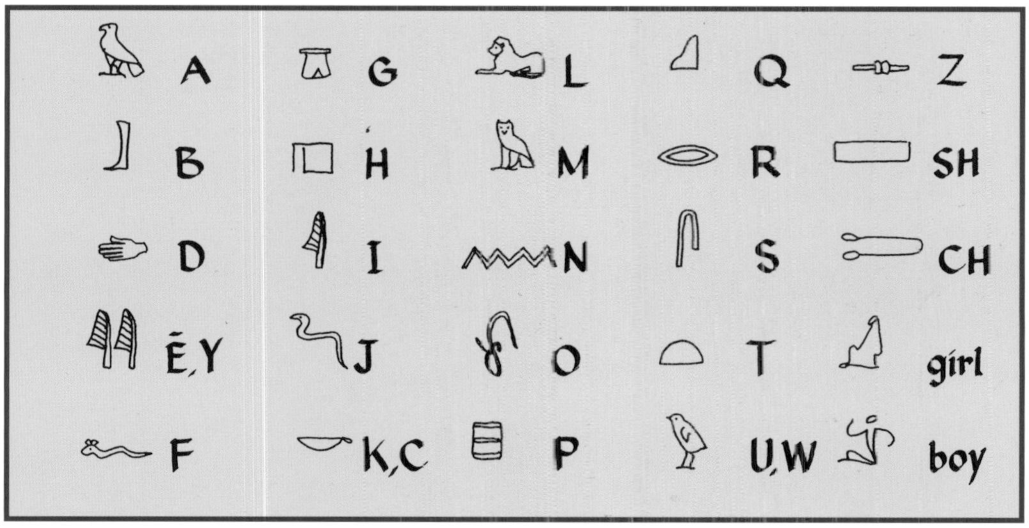

JO(A)N   girl

STEPH(E)N   boy

𓄿	A	𓎼	G	𓃭	L	𓈎	Q	𓏤	Z
𓃀	B	�	H	𓅓	M	𓂋	R	𓈖	SH
𓂧	D	𓇋	I	𓈖	N	𓋴	S	𓎡	CH
𓇌	Ê,Y	𓆓	J	𓅱	O	𓏏	T	𓁧	girl
𓆑	F	𓎡	K,C	𓊪	P	𓅭	U,W	𓀔	boy

Cuneiform, on page 74, appears to be austere, geometric, and abstract in contrast with Egyptian hieroglyphics which are poetic and fascinating... almost alive in the stylized drawings of feathers, birds, animals, and plants. According to ancient Egyptians it was the God Thoth who created writing and bestowed it as a gift on humankind. It remained little changed for 3500 years, though the signs increased from 700 to 5,000. In contrast to the Sumerians, the Egyptian's writing system expressed everything they wished to record. Jean-Francois Champollion penetrated the secrets of the writing in 1822 by deciphering the Rosetta Stone found in 1799. The history of Egypt might have remained largely unknown had we not been able to decipher tomb writings.

Tamara Bower has used hieroglyphics in the story ***The   Shipwrecked Tailor,*** Atheneum, NY, 2000.

THE EGYPTIAN PYRAMID

THE EGYPTIAN PYRAMID

Materials: White or buff railroad board, ruler, scissors, pencil, paint that makes a sandy color: white, yellow, brown mix, sponges, rectangle printing material, glue, paper clips, masking tape.

The pyramid is a geometric form: the equilateral triangle with four triangular sides.

1. Decide on the size of the pyramid. Find the pattern on page 81. Double or triple the size when you copy it.

2. After copying the pyramid pattern, trace around it on the railroad board. Cut out the equilateral triangle.

3. Score along all triangle lines with a sharp point such as your scissor's point. Fold wherever there are scores. Put the pyramid sides together to make sure they are going to connect. Mark the horizontal line of each triangle with a pencil so the finishing textures are horizontal.

4. Mix the sandy colors a little, but not too much as you want the pyramid to have several color textures. You should have something rectangular that is to scale with the pyramid. In order to print the stones, a 10" pyramid would have a rectangle 1/2" x 1". It might be a sponge piece, a foam piece, or a cardboard piece. It should be easily gripped.

5. Dip the rectangle piece into the shallow paint dish and stamp "stones"onto the pyramid surface or brush the paint onto the rectangle. Do this on all pyramid surfaces but leave the bottom plain. Let the paint dry.

6. Glue the flaps together on one side and weight it or keep glue secured with light masking tape. This is the tricky part. After drying time, carefully remove the securing tape and admire the handsome pyramid.

More than 80 pyramids of different shapes and sizes have been discovered in Egypt. The most famous is the Great Pyramid of Khufu at Giza. It is one of the Seven Wonders of the Ancient World. It was built in 2570 B.C. It was covered with limestone, a hard shiny surface, and had a capstone of gold that reflected the sun's rays. Later, pyramids had stepped sides that were made smooth. The burial chamber was inside the shape. By the late Old Kingdom it was clear that pyramids took too much labor and material. Pharaohs began to be buried in rock-cut tombs in the Valley of the Kings. It was here the Tutankhamen tomb was discovered in 1922 by Howard Carter.

Jan M. Mike has written ***Gift of the Nile,*** Troll Assoc. 1999.

An Introduction to Islam

Born in the seventh century A.D. in **Saudi Arabia**, Islam is a monotheistic religion focusing on the glorification of the One Supreme Being, Allah, and around a Holy Book, the Qur'an revealed between 610 and 632 A.D. to the Prophet Muhammad. Islam was founded at a time when moral and spiritual laxity was at its height in the region of Mecca and further north in Medina. Muhammad's followers and successors soon spread the word of Islam in the surrounding areas and beyond Arabia. To Muslims, the followers of Islam, their religion became a way of life, forming and guiding their entire culture and society.

The Five Pillars of Islam are known as duties and together support the structure of Islam. **The Qur'an,** which means "recitation," has 114 chapters. Muslims believe that it expresses precisely the word of God.

The Shahada means "bearing witness" and is a declaration of faith that there is only one God (Allah) and that Muhammad is his messenger. **The Salat** is the ritual prayer, said five times a day while a person kneels in the direction of the Ka'bah in Mecca.

wooden holder of the Qur'an

The Zakat is a form of charity and is 2.5% of one's wealth. The **Sawm** is the fast from sunrise to sunset during the month of Ramadan. The Fifth and final pillar is **Hajji**, a special pilgrimage to Mecca which brings millions of Muslims together for common worship. It is expected that all adult Muslims must try to make the journey once in their lifetime if physically and financially able. Some symbols of Islam are shown below:

mosque   **minaret**

prayer beads

prayer mats

Ka'bah

ART IN THE ISLAMIC WORLD

Islamic design has a spiritual importance because it is considered by Muslims to be a way for humans to reflect the glory of nature as created by Allah. From early days the idea of portraying humans and animals was rejected as idol worship.

FIVE CHARACTERISTICS OF ISLAMIC ART

1.**Tessellations:** Squares, triangles, and hexagons are shapes that will fit together with all sides connecting. These are called tessellations. They imply infinity.

2. **Complex Star Polygons:** Before computers, these complex patterns were drawn with a ruler and compass.

3. **Linear Repeat Patterns:** These are often borders around blocks of pattern. They add a rich effect. Often several borders are combined.

4. **Arabesques:** These are plant-world in form but stylized. Often the arabesque weaves in and out and around things. The arabesque symbolizes the organized earth with its underlying structures.

5. **Calligraphy in the Arabic Alphabet:** Calligraphy in Arabic is referred to as "the geometry of line", line meaning writing or letters. Since the rise of Islam, calligraphy has been a major art form. Numerous manuscripts have survived describing the preparation or inks, colors and paper. Here is the essential calligraphed form which reads "al-salaam" which means peace.
This is the heart of Islamic art. It is the most important of all unifying characteristics and is, to this day, the most treasured and revered art form. It is through calligraphy that the Divine Intention is expressed explicitly. Arabic is read from right to left and the alphabet has 28 letters.

THE EYE OF GOOD FORTUNE

THE EYE OF GOOD FORTUNE

Materials: Light cardboard, circle templates such as lids, cup tops or bottoms etc., pencil, scissors, dark blue, light blue and white paint, small brush, strong black marker, hole punch (making bricks, like the photo, with plaster of paris is optional).

1. Think about how the "eyes" are going to be used: a necklace, glued to a surface, strung on yarn, put above a doorway. Draw around the circles. Do not cut them out yet.

2. Paint the outside color dark blue. It can vary in thickness, but remember that three more colors will be applied. Next paint the paper white or leave a space and paint light blue. After all the colors have dried, mark the light blue circle as the eye's pupil with a black marker. Now carefully cut out each eye circle.

3. Punch a hole at the top of the eye and put it to the use you have planned.

In near Eastern countries such as Turkey people wear the "eye" or put it in their environment, as if more eyes indicate more protection from anything undesirable. The eyes are made of glass. Jewelry such as bracelets, rings, necklaces and earrings, all include the lucky eye looking out. When constructing a wall or a house, glass eyes are put in the brick material to keep bad luck away from the area. Just as Africans wear their *gris gris* charms and Mexicans have their colorful *Ojo de Dios* yarn objects, the blue eye serves the same purpose in parts of the Arab world.

Another explanation for "the evil eye" is that the evil gaze is about envy. Inciting the envy of others can be a dangerous thing. Fear of the evil eye has caused some people to do just about anything to avoid being enviable in any way. The charm is meant to deflect the evil back onto its source.

MOSAIC TILES

MOSAIC TILES: AN ANCIENT ART

Materials: One of each 10" x 10" and 12" x 12" manila cardboard or other light cardboard, ruler, pencil, acrylic paint, brushes, glue, sharp scissors, clear acrylic spray, powdered grout, water, sponge.

1. Look at pattern ideas on page 7. Draw the design on a practice paper.

2. Now, draw the design onto a smaller cardboard piece. Paint the design. Let it dry.

3. Spray paint the design with acrylic sealer. Several applications will give the mosaic a shiny ceramic-like shine. Let it dry.

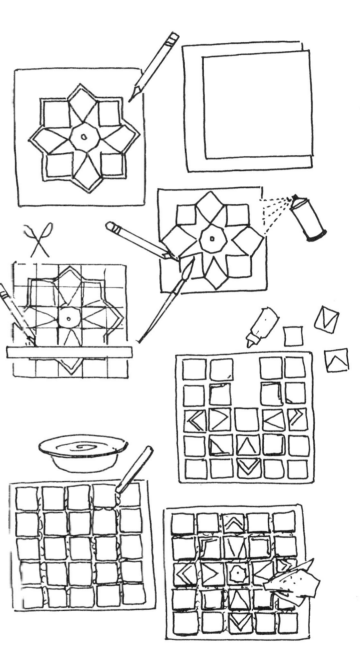

4. With a pencil and ruler lightly mark the design into 5" equal squares. Cut out the squares.

5. Reassemble the squares on the larger cardboard piece. Leave narrow spaces between each square. The space will hold the "grout" which is like a cement. Glue the squares in place.

6. Mix water into powdered grout and mix until smooth. With a blunt knife or craft stick carefully work the grout into spaces between the squares.

7. Gently remove excess grout with a damp (but not wet) sponge. Rinse the sponge frequently in clear water to remove all grout residue from the shiny mosaic tile.

This art form is one of the most ancient of the Middle and Near East dating back as early as 2000 B.C. Assyrians and Babylonians used enameled brick to decorate their palaces. Lapis blue and turquoise are the most common colors The process of making tiles today is almost the same as in ancient times.

THREE MINARETS

THREE MINARETS

Materials: Any boxes or tubes that are the correct scale (our biggest is 6" x 6" with a 12" tube our longest), plain paper, markers, crayons, oil pastels, glue, scissors, ruler, pencil. Paper strips, flour and water for making papier–mache'. Spools, glitter, buttons and any decorative trims are optional.

In researching this project over one hundred minarets were studied and composite forms were created using authentic but easily replicated patterns.

1. Gather the cardboard forms: salt, oatmeal, paper tubes were all used for the "blue minaret" and the simpler red one. Stack the boxes. A hole may have to be cut to put tubes through lids.

2. Papier–mache' for strength: Make a paste of 1 part flour to 1 1/2 parts water. Tear newspaper strips. Start making your minaret sturdy by dipping the strips Let the minaret dry overnight.

3. Cut paper strips that will fit around the boxes. They will be colored with classic designs. Think about balconies, arches and windows as they are all possible features. Think very hard about the roof. A conical form is the easiest. How will it be attached? This is the time when these architectural features are planned and added.

4. Design the colors and paper that will fit around the minaret base. Review the geometric patterns on page 7. After coloring each of the papers glue them around the minaret section. Add balconies and railings. Make a cone for the roof and decide how it is going to be attached. This should have been thought about during the papier-mache' process. After every beautiful colored and designed paper surface is in place, stand back...the minaret should be something beautiful and interesting to behold just as it is for Islamic worshippers.

5. The brown square minaret is the same process using square boxes exclusively.

The minaret is a high column designed as a platform for the muezzin (mujadhin) to call people to prayer *(the Adhan)*. It can stand alone or be part of a mosque. Angela Wood has written ***Muslim Mosque,*** Gareth Stevens Pub., Milwaukee, WI., 2000.

Painted Patterns

PAINTED PATTERNS

Materials: As many 4" square tiles as needed. Special paint that dries hard on tile surface: DeltaCeramdecoro and PermEnamel Surface Conditioner®, a variety of brushes, water, pencil, paper for design work, grid for geometrics, page 85.

The popular and beautiful Spanish and Mexican tiles probably originated in southern Spain with the Moors, victors in peacefully occupying the south of Spain for several hundred years. Variations of the designs continue to cover walls, arches, roofs, and floors of mosques in every part of the Muslim world.

1. Clean the surface of the tile with a damp cloth. Any plain colored tile works well. Brush on the Surface Conditioner as step one if the tiles are to be used beyond a display.
2. With a 4" square paper and pencil, design the tile. Think about the corner making a pattern of its own when the tiles are put together. Here are some traditional Muslim designs:

3. Let the tiles dry (about an hour) and glue them to the surface. Add grout to finish the tiled surface.

Tessellation has been discussed as one of the elements of design. Any shape made by combining triangles can be tessellated. A study of the architecture and sculpture and most art forms in the Arab world is rich with simple and complicated ceramic tiles.

A Prayer Rug

A Prayer Rug

***Materials: Heavy white school paper 3' x 5', pencil, ruler, Jiffy Foam®
for print-making, paint, markers.***

1. Measure and cut the school paper to a rectangle
3' x 5'. Design the borders on a smaller practice paper.

2. Mark the borders with a ruler and pencil.
The inside of the rug should be at least 2' x 3'.

3. Paint the borders and the center. Keep in
mind the colors you are going to paint for contrast.
See page 7 and 51 for border patterns.

4. Study shapes common to Islamic art. See page 7.
Cut the shapes from cardboard or Jiffy Foam for
a clean print. Prepare the paint palette (paper plate or
Styrofoam meat tray). Brush on the paint or
stamp it. Try the print on scrap paper. Fill the
borders with the repeat painted print design.

5. Cut out shapes for the center. The Ka'bah is often
part of the rug design; also common is the image of a
minaret. Trace around the paper pattern and paint the
center of the rug with great care. The rug's central
images could be painted on separate paper and glued in place.

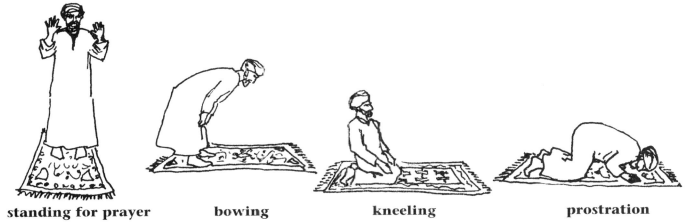

| standing for prayer | bowing | kneeling | prostration |

**Prayer mats are laid on a surface to insure cleanliness. A Muslim does not have
to kneel on a prayer mat but some have favorite prayer mats that they keep
with them. A mat may be a woolen carpet or made of straw or cotton. Prayer
mats often have geometric patterns or sometimes pictures of famous mosques,
but they never show images of people.**

THE HAND OF GOOD LUCK

THE HAND OF GOOD LUCK

Materials: White manila folder or poster board or aluminum 6" x 12", a disposable foil cookie sheet, blue bead or button, white glue, black, grey and white acrylic or tempera paint, sponges, pencil, hole punch, patterns on page 73.

1. Lay the hand on the rectangular surface. Trace around it with a pencil, indenting the foil. Look at the photograph. Notice that three of the hands have fat fingers and the big hand has cut out fingers. Decide the way you want your hand to be. Cut out your hand.

2. The hands have a decorative "relief" of dots, curves, flowers, stars, outlines. Draw the designs on the hand-shape with a pencil. Next, reinforce the pencil lines with white glue applied from a tip that makes a controlled line. Experiment on a scrap of paper. You do not want a big glob of glue. Rather, you are drawing with glue. Let the glue dry overnight. The big hand has black marker outlining the designs. Next brush on blue paint. Both looks are authentic.

3. Put white and black paint the size of a dime on a paint dish. Use a small dry sponge piece dipped in the black and white paint and gently sponge over the glue lines. It should look patchy. Glue on the blue bead or button.

hamsa

4. Punch a hole at the wrist for hanging over a door on a string or a nail. These hands are commonly found in many places.

The downward-hanging hamsa (Arabic) hand is usually open with thumbs on each side. An alternative name for the charm is "Hand of Fatima" named for Muhammad's daughter. The hands can be suspended above doorways, included in wall paintings, and incorporated into architecture. Hamsa is also the root word for the number five in Arabic. Whether engraved or carved, realistic or stylized, it is rare when some form of the eye or hand is not displayed in an Arabic dwelling. Often it is in the form of jewelry or embroidery. People most susceptible to the evil eye or who are most likely to wear the hand charm are brides, pregnant women, and babies. *(continued on page 81)*

A TRADITIONAL BAG

A TRADITIONAL BAG

Materials: Heavy white school paper 30" x 15" folded in half, 5-6 yarn colors (each tassel has 3 feet of yarn), buttons, bells, beads, markers or crayons, ruler, pencil, glue, stapler, scissors, big-eyed needle.

1. Cut the rectangle of paper and fold in half so your paper surface is 15" x 15". Using a ruler and pencil, plan a design which will cover the paper with color and geometric patterns. Design some bands for glued buttons. These were woven bags and used traditional zig-zag lines, diamonds, and triangles. See page 7 for ideas.

2. Color your bag and add the decorative touches.

3. Make the tassels by winding the yarn around a 3" cardboard piece. Cut the bottom of the tassel and wind one of the pieces around the top, thus making a knob. Thread the yarn through the needle-eye and push it through the wrapped section, securing the wrapping.

4. Place the tassels evenly on the bag. Staple the top row. Glue the rows in the middle. Put a book weight on the glued tassels overnight to dry.

5. Glue or staple the open side of the bag. Add a 24" handle of braided yarn or a double 1 1/2" paper band. Color the paper band; then glue the sides together and staple to each side of the bag.

These handsome bags were traditionally used as containers on camels and donkeys. They were also hung near the door on the wall of the wedding house ready to receive gifts.

ARABIC CALLIGRAPHY

ARABIC CALLIGRAPHY

Materials: Paper, pencil, Arabic alphabet on page 74, any additional art supplies for Arabic writing.

Guide to the Arabic alphabet

Arabic is written from right to left.

Each Arabic letter has one sound and each sound has one letter.

The 28 letters use 14 shapes mixed with 0-3 dots above or below them.

We will concentrate on these three.

Writing a Name in the Arabic alphabet

1. Print a name on a piece of paper with a blank written for each letter in the name. Number each sound in your name. For example: In English two letters often share one sound

        Th   sh   ry   ey

Put a copy of the "English to Arabic" page in front of you. Look down the list of English letters on the page, checking to be sure you are choosing the right SOUND for each numbered letter or pair of letters above, and write the Arabic letters in the blanks below, beginning on the far right:

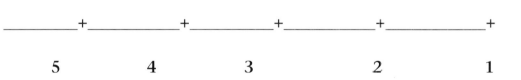

_____+_____+_____+_____+_____+_____+

    5   4   3   2   1

Connectors are used to give the calligraphy fluidity. This step is not being included as connectors come in middle, initial and final forms (almost 60 shapes) which is overwhelming to most beginners. The purpose of the study-and-do activity is to become acquainted with the alphabet and to produce a few words.

Calligraphy is an art form in the Islamic culture. It is incorporated into every aspect of life: furnishings, clothing, architecture, and household objects. Because the Muslim faith is a complete way of life, the religious values are often expressed in the form of calligraphied scriptures or wise sayings from the Qu'ran that blend into everything and are found everywhere.

PAPER CHAINS

Paper Chains

Materials: Colored paper, scissors, pencil, glue or tape, patterns on page 75-78. Paint and markers optional.

1. Cut the paper into sections 5"– 7" wide and as long as needed.

2. Fold your paper strip accordion-style into three to four sections. For a longer paper chain add more paper strips. Cutting this many is about the best a scissors can cut.

3. Choose a pattern from the pattern page or design your own.

4. If you want to color or paint your paper, do it now. Suggestions are to cut some out of wrapping or wallpaper or sponge paint some with color dabs. Let the paper strip dry before proceeding.

5. Refold your dry paper strip. *Trace the design onto your folded paper strip, making sure the design extends to the folded sides so that when it is cut out the shapes **are connected.***

6. Secure your paper for cutting by slipping a paper clip onto a section which will be cut away.

7. Repeat as many of the same or different designs as you wish. Fasten ends of your paper chains together with tape or glue.

Paper chains can be used as borders for displays, book marker patterns, gift tags, any theme presentation that might need scenery motifs (when enlarged), invitations to a theme event, and stencils for a variety of purposes.

Three Sumerian Chariots - *(continued from page 15)*
The Warrior Chariot

1. Cut four wheels from cardboard 3" in diameter. Paint and marker them to look like the real Sumerian wooden wheels. Stick two 3" dowels through the two sets of wheels.

2. Cut a cardboard pattern like the one on page 81, doubling it in size. Add the marker lines which were often bronze strips. Paint them a second color after you have painted the body of the chariot a wood color.

The Sumerians are credited with inventing the wheel more than 6000 years ago. Heavy loads and passengers were transported in animal-drawn sledges, wagons, chariots, boats or by pack animals. As early as 2800 B.C. there is an image of a sledge with four wheels. Wheeled vehicles such as our first two projects have been found in royal tombs. Possibly the potter's wheel is also a Sumerian invention.

Cuneiform - *(continued from page 25)*

The pictures were put on prepared clay pieces perhaps 10,000 years ago by Sumerians. By 2500 B.C. pictograms had become more simplified with curves, triangles, and straight lines. This was called cuneiform (wedge shaped). The importance of cuneiform came when the symbols were used to show sounds of words.

Cuneiform was NOT a language. It was a technique for writing used by many peoples. Babylonian scribes cut ends of reeds into points and pressed them into damp clay. In 1846 experts learned how to "read" dried cuneiform clay tablets. They told mythical stories about economic dealings, wise sayings, and the history of these amazing ancient people.

Shabti Figures -*(continued from page 29)*
Every Egyptian was required to do some farming and irrigation work in the next life. Rich Egyptians paid workers to do this for them. Heaven was called the Field of Reeds and the dead Egyptian was again expected to work for Osiris. From the earliest tombs the wealthy were buried with clay worker-figures called "shabti". The Book of the Dead has this inscription:

"Oh shabti, if the deceased is called upon to do any work required there,... you will say, 'Here I am, I will do it.' "

In the New Kingdom (1500 B.C.) one shabti was enough. By 1000 B.C. 401 shabti were buried...one for each day of the year plus 36 bosses who carried whips to keep the workers on task.

Toys from the Tombs - *(continued from page 31)*
Tomb paintings throughout Egyptian history show people playing board games. Egyptian children played with homemade toys such as these leather balls, the wooden horse, and the fabric doll. There are paintings of boys playing soldiers and girls holding dolls. Some dolls were made of wood with string for hair. This doll is patterned after a toy found in a young Egyptian princess' tomb.

Scarabs - *(continued from page 33)*
The Scarab Pin: *Materials are dough or air drying clay, the 4 Egyptian colors of paint, brush.*
Follow the procedure of the winged scarab.
After baking, paint the scarab.

The Scarab Gift Bag: *Materials are a purchased paper gift bag, pencil, ruler, paint, brushes, black marker.*

1. With your ruler and pencil mark the design on the paper bag. Paint the pattern on the bag.
2. Go over the dried paint dividing lines with black marker. Use a scarab template on page 74.

Two Stitchery Scarabs: *Materials are a piece of handwoven fabric aged with dark tea bags (Dab used soggy tea bags on fabric. Blend. Rinse in cold water.), embroidery hoop, colorful yarn like crewel, a big-eyed needle, scissors, matte frames, masking tape.*

1. The simple embroidery stitches are a running stitch (red frame in photograph), chain, satin, French knot, and blanket stitch. Design the scarab on paper with colored marker. Be creative and use lots of color.
2. Iron the stitchery when it is finished. Tape the edges to the back of a matte board.

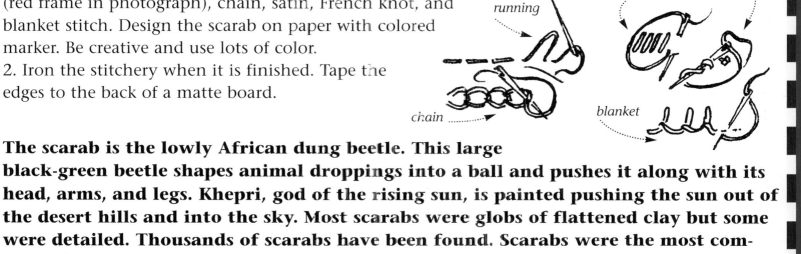

running
satin
French knot
chain
blanket

The scarab is the lowly African dung beetle. This large black-green beetle shapes animal droppings into a ball and pushes it along with its head, arms, and legs. Khepri, god of the rising sun, is painted pushing the sun out of the desert hills and into the sky. Most scarabs were globs of flattened clay but some were detailed. Thousands of scarabs have been found. Scarabs were the most common of Egyptian amulets called good-luck charms. Egyptians were burying charms with their dead 7,000 years ago. Scarabs and the Eye of Horus are the amulets found most frequently in burial places.

The Aten Crown: *Materials are white or yellow railroad board 18" x 22", 6" paper bowl, flour, water, paper strips for papier mache', paper clips, red, gold, blue, green and turquoise paint, brushes, scissors.*

1. Cut out the crown. The tall forms are 7" each and 16" tall from the crown base. Look at the photograph.
2. Place the paper bowl in front and attach to the crown with papier-mache' strips. Let dry overnight. Paint the crown gold, the sun red, and the trim around the sun and tall forms blue. Adjust the size to fit the wearer's head.

King Tut Headdress: *Materials are half of a piece of gold railroad board 14" x 22". If gold cardboard is not available, spray paint white with gold paint, blue construction paper, glue, stapler, scissors. Patterns on pages 80 and 84.*

1. Enlarge serpent and headdress patterns to twice the size. Trace both sides onto posterboard. Cut them out.
2. With a scissor point, score along dotted lines of headdress and serpent.
3. Glue blue paper to serpent's head and belly. Draw eyes. Fold head on dotted lines.
4. Cut 1" blue paper strips for stripes for sides and top of headdress. Glue in place, trimming excess along the edges.
5. Fold sides down. Staple flaps. Adjust headband to size. Staple.
6. Curl serpent gently around pencil. Staple bottom end to crown. Arch serpent upward and staple or glue to center of the headdress.

Egyptian kings and queens wore a range of royal headdresses. By wearing one of these crowns the King was transformed into a god.

The White Crown: **Osiris is often depicted wearing the Atef, the white crown with serpents and feathers. Many tombs show dead pharaohs wearing it as they have "joined with Osiris" in the next world.**

The Blue Crown: **This headwear was like a helmet covered in gold studs or discs. It is sometimes called the "War Crown" as it was worn in and out of battle. Queens are painted wearing a similar blue helmet crown.**

The Sun Crown: **This crown was worn by Akhenaton, the Pharaoh that worshipped one god: Aten, the sun. His queen Nefertiti's famous sculpted head is shown on page 36 wearing a crown unique to her.**

Harp: *Materials are cardboard 15" x 12" for top piece, two more cardboard pieces for strengthening that are the same size cut as crescents, 6 brass brads, gold, red, green, white, blue, yellow, and orange paint and brushes, 80" of monofilament or 4" rubber bands, paring knife or exacto blade and strong scissors. Pattern on page 82.*

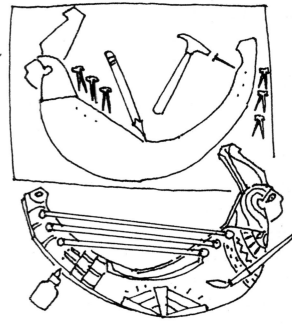

1. Using the enlarged pattern, trace it on the cardboard. Puncture the outline with a knife on a soft surface such as a carpet. Laying the top pattern on the cardboard, cut out at least one under-crescent shape and two if you need more strength. The top harp can be painted at any time.
2. Glue the cardboard layers together and let dry with a heavy object on top.
3. Hammer six holes marked on the pattern. Place the brads in each hole. Notch rubber bands around each brad. Is the harp strong enough for the tension? Use monofilament if the harp buckles with the rubber bands because of too much tension.

Clapping rhythms were important sounds for dance and song. Flutes, harps, and lutes provided music. Both men and women played instruments. The sistrum rattle was used in temple ceremonies, especially honoring Hathor, goddess of music.

HAMSA HANDS

EGYPTIAN CARTOUCHE

ARABIC ALPHABET

ش س ز ر ذ د خ ح ج ث ت ب ا

shin sin zin ra dhal dal kha ha jim theh teh beh alif

ي و ه ن م ل ك ق ف غ ع ظ ط ض ص

yeh waw heh nun mim lam kaf qaf feh ghain ain DHa Ta Dad sad

ARABIC NUMERALS

٩ ٨ ٧ ٦ ٥ ٤ ٣ ٢ ١ ٠

9 8 7 6 5 4 3 2 1 0

ENGLISH TO ARABIC

ă	ا	f,v	ف	n	ن	t	ت
ā	ـِي	h	ح	ŏ	ـُ	u,w	و
b	ب	ĭ	ـ	ō	ـُو	x	كس
c,k,g	ك	ī	ايي	p	ب	z	ز
d	د	j	ج	q	ق	th	ث
ě	ـ	l	ل	r	د	sh	ش
ē,y	ي	m	م	s	س	ph	ف

SCARAB PATTERNS

74

MUMMIES

A mummy is a dead body that has been preserved by drying. Ancient Egyptians developed artificial techniques for preserving their dead in this way. They decided that the dead needed their bodies in the next life. Preserving a body took 70 days. First the body was washed, then the brain was removed through the nose, and then the internal organs were removed, embalmed, and stored in canopic jars. The mummies were wrapped several times. Here are the stages of unwrapping a royal advisor:

The mummy is wrapped in a shawl.

The linen-covered face is covered with a mask and collar.

The linen is covered with a hardened resin.

The removal of more linens exposes rich jewels.

After more bandages are removed the corpse has another fine collar, bracelets, anklets and good-luck charms in the bandages.

PAPER
CHAIN
EGYPTIAN
COLUMN

EYE OF HORUS

PAPER CHAIN PATTERNS

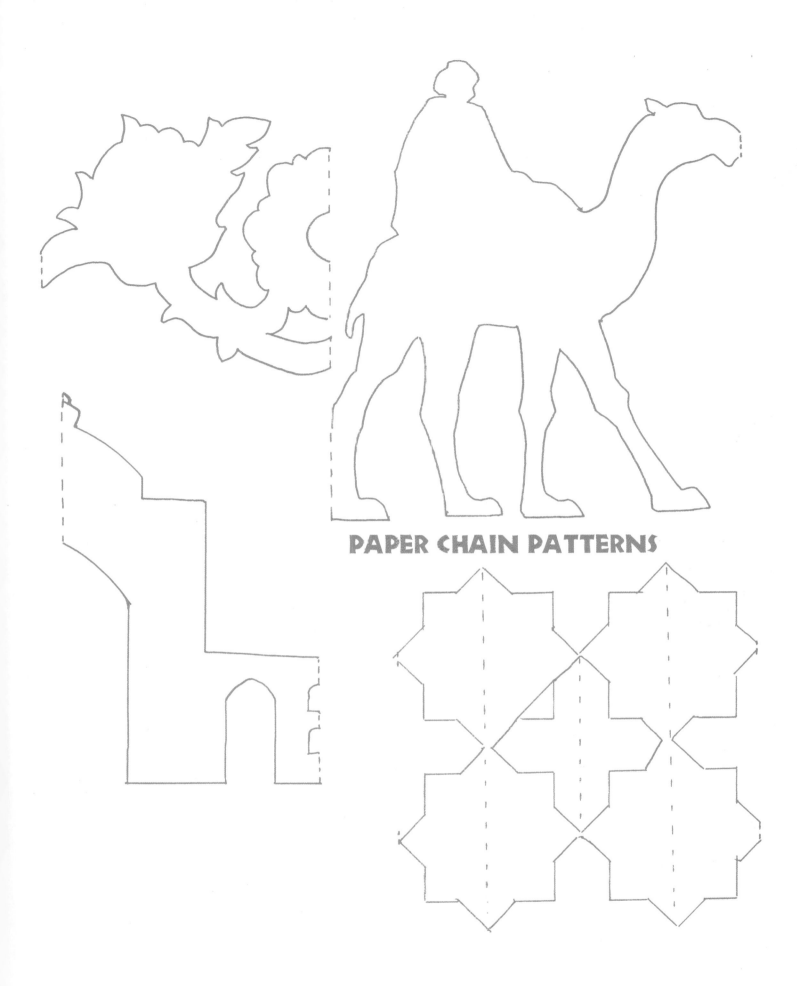

PAPER CHAIN PATTERNS

PAPER CHAIN PATTERNS

Animals continued from page 41

Animals were important in Egyptian life. Favorite pets were cats, dogs, monkeys, and gazelles. The importance of animals can be seen by the animal heads many of the gods and goddesses wore. When people died in ancient Egypt their bodies were mummified. To help prevent a body from decaying, the internal organs were removed and placed inside special containers known as canopic jars. The four god's heads were always used as stoppers: the ape or baboon's head oversaw the lungs; the man's head oversaw the liver; the hawk's head oversaw the intestines; and the jackal's head oversaw the stomach. Deborah Norse Lattimore has written ***The Winged Cat,*** Harper Collins, NY, 1992.

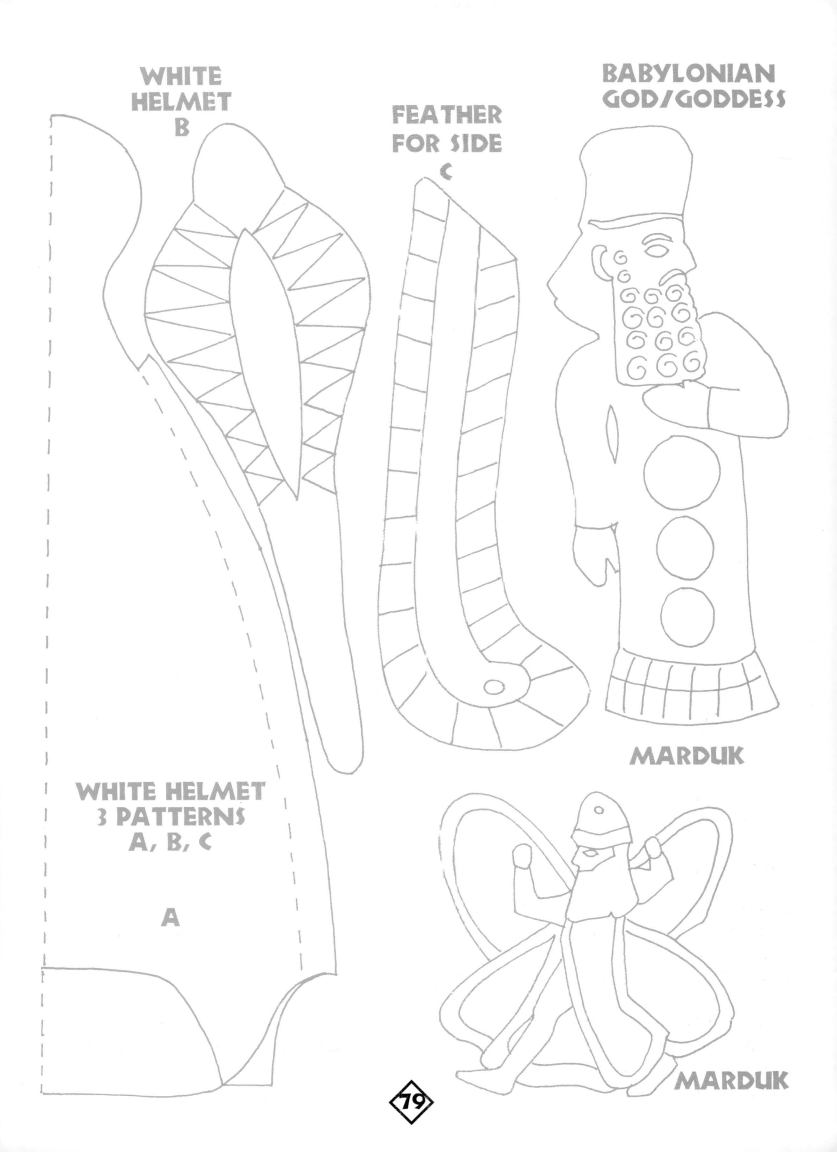

WHITE
HELMET
B

FEATHER
FOR SIDE
C

BABYLONIAN
GOD/GODDESS

WHITE HELMET
3 PATTERNS
A, B, C

A

MARDUK

MARDUK

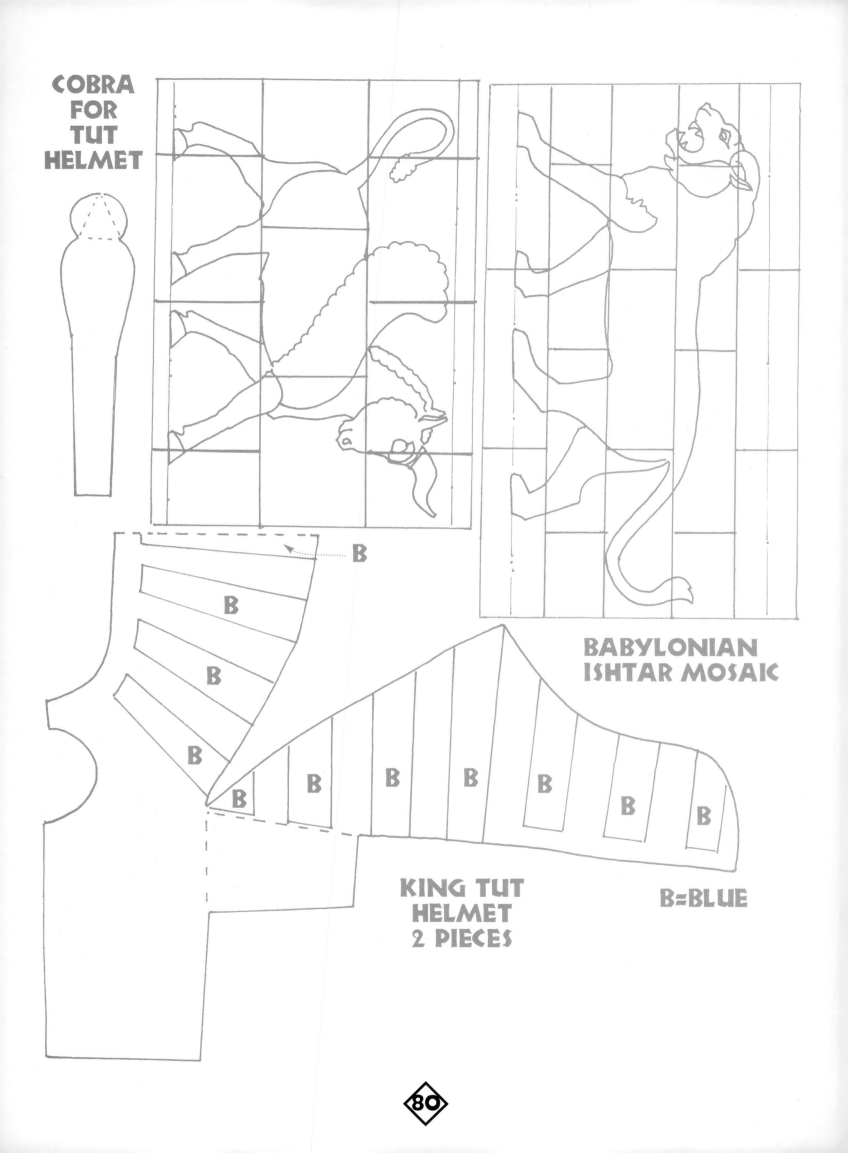

COBRA
FOR
TUT
HELMET

B

B

B

B

B

B

B

B

B

B

B

B

BABYLONIAN
ISHTAR MOSAIC

KING TUT
HELMET
2 PIECES

B=BLUE

The Hand of Good Luck -
(continued from page 63) **The open blue hand on a pink arch stone in the photograph appears on the keystone of an arched doorway of the Alhambra Palace in Granada, Spain. The five fingers represent the Pillars of Islam. Shi'ite Muslims carry the silver hand in processions. The smaller hands are good-luck charms in the Middle East. The turquoise bead offers protection against the "evil eye."**

Shelamith Levey Oppenheim and Ed Young have written ***Iblis,*** Harcourt Brace and Co. San Diego, 1994.

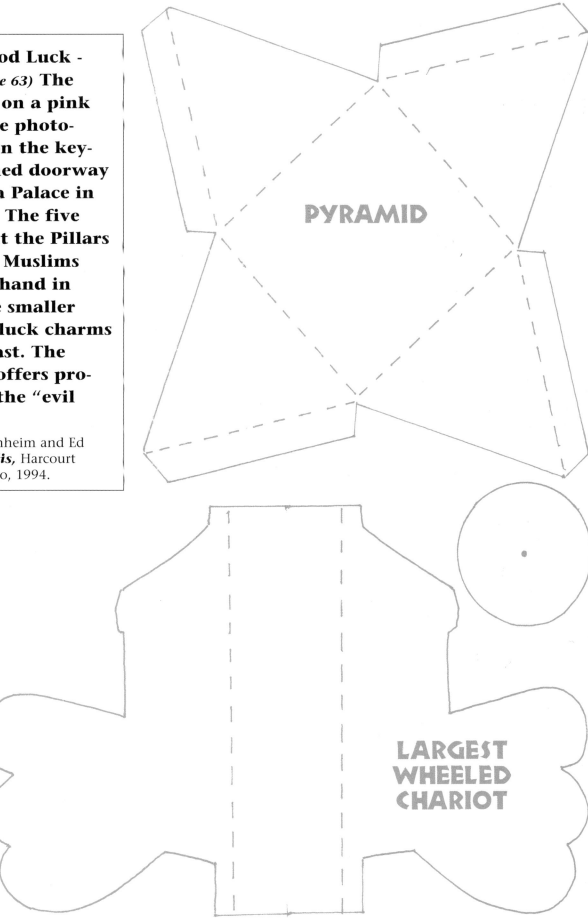

PYRAMID

LARGEST
WHEELED
CHARIOT

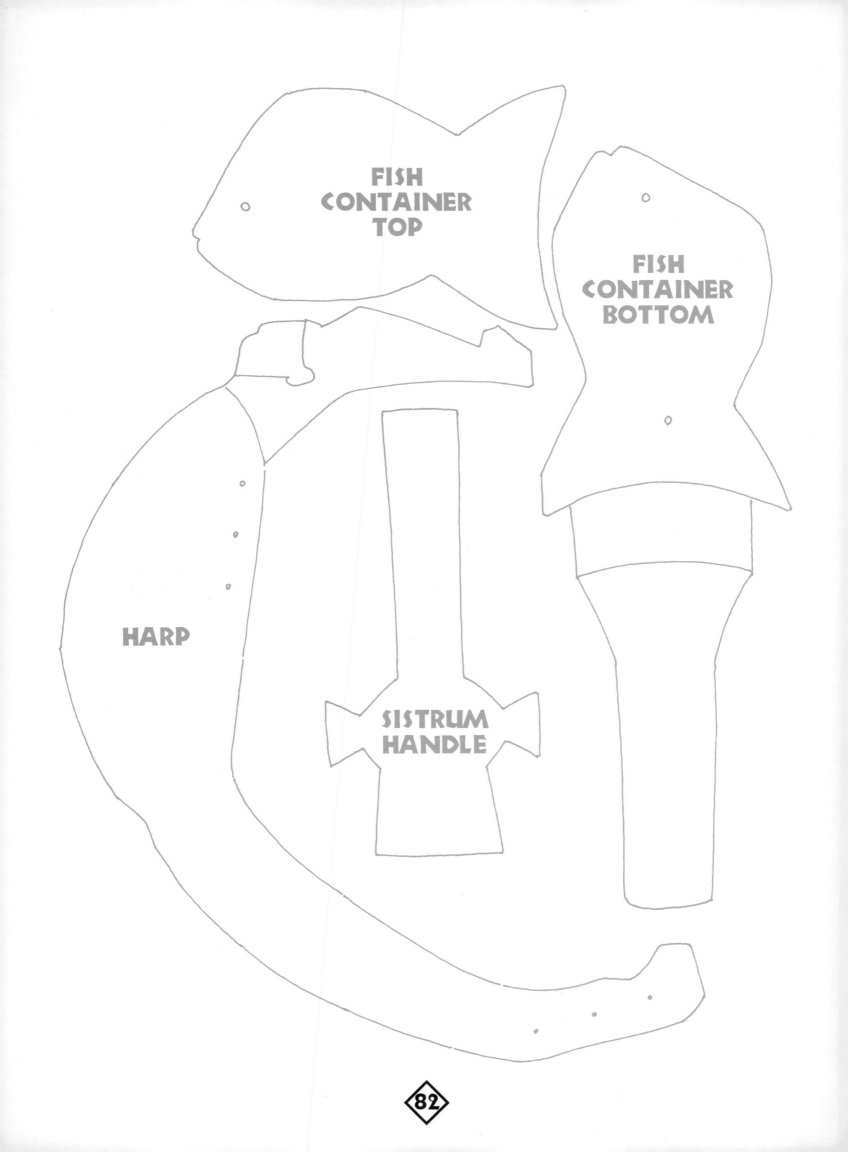

FISH
CONTAINER
TOP

FISH
CONTAINER
BOTTOM

HARP

SISTRUM
HANDLE

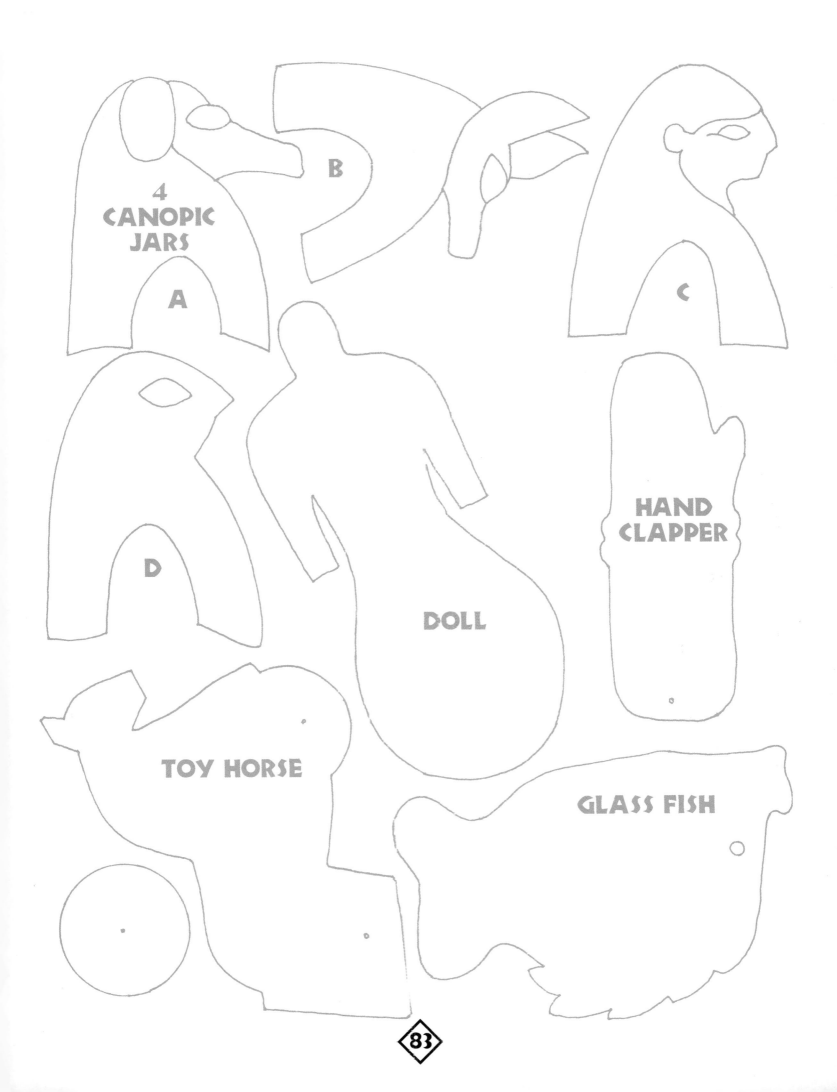

4
CANOPIC
JARS

B

A

C

D

DOLL

HAND
CLAPPER

TOY HORSE

GLASS FISH

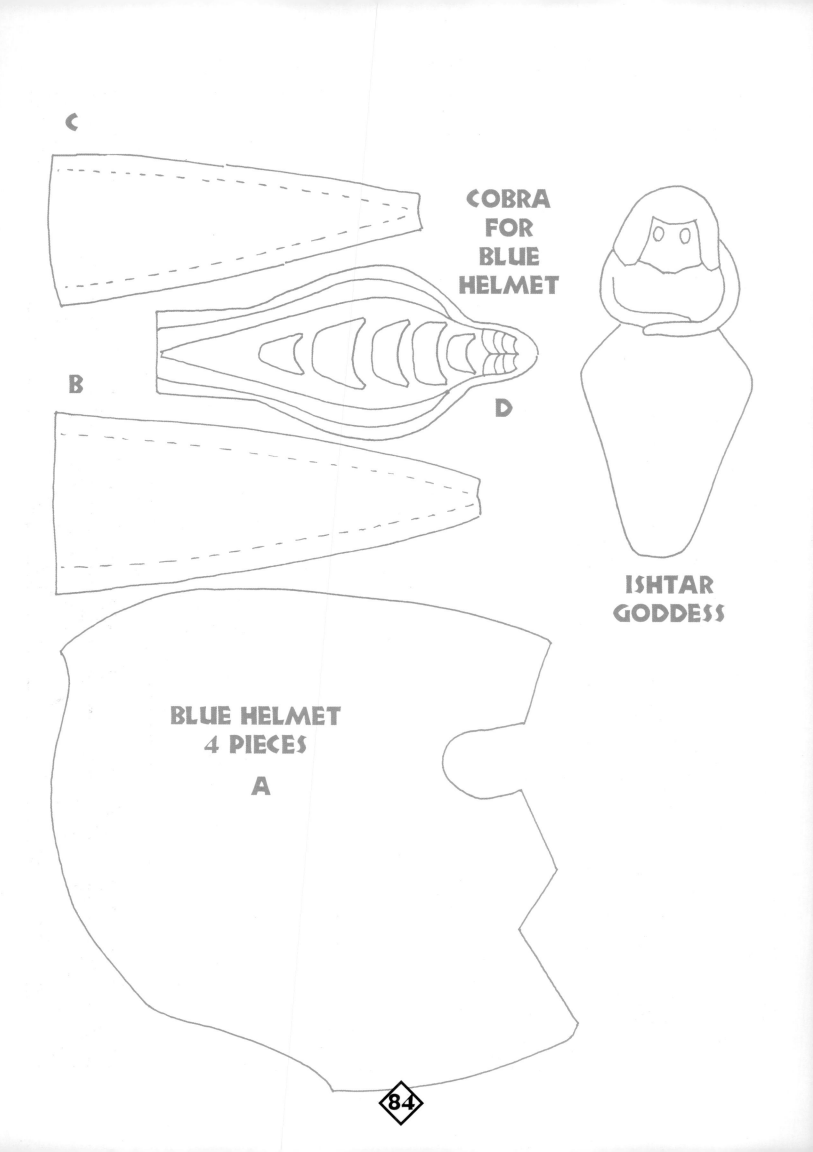

C

COBRA
FOR
BLUE
HELMET

B

D

ISHTAR
GODDESS

BLUE HELMET
4 PIECES

A

INDEX

BIBLIOGRAPHY AND ACKNOWLEDGEMENTS

Staff from the University of Utah Center for Middle East Studies reviewed and corrected the Islam section. George Ellington and June Marvel are gratefully acknowledged.

MESOPOTAMIA

Foster, Leila Merrill, *The Sumerians,* Franklin Watts, NY, 1990.

Malam, John, *Mesopotamia and the Fertile Crescent,* Steck-Vaughn, Austin, Texas, 1999.

Moss, Carol, *Science in Ancient Mesopotamia,* Franklin Watts, NY, 1988.

Nardo, Don, *The Assyrian Empire: World History Series,* Lucent Books, Inc. San Diego, 1998.

Scarre, Chris, *Timelines of the Ancient World, A Visual Chronology from the Origins of Life to AD 1500,* Smithsonian, Doring Kindersley, London, 1993.

Service, Pamela F., *Ancient Mesopotamia,* Benchmark Books, Tarrytown, NY ,1999.

Wilson, Bernice, *Art of the Ancient Mediterranean World,* International Encyclopedia of Art, Cynthia Parzych Pub., Inc., NY, 1996.

EGYPT

Cavendish, Marshall, *History of the Ancient and Medieval World, Mesopotamia and Egypt: Volume 2,* Marshall Cavendish, NY, 1996.

Harris, Geraldine and Delia Pemberton, *Illustrated Encyclopedia of Ancient Egypt,* Peter Bedrick Books, Chicago, 1999.

Hart, George, *Ancient Egypt: Eyewitness Books,* Knopf, NY, 1990.

ISLAM

Ahsan, M.M., *Muslim Festivals,* Rourke Enterprises, Vero Beach, Ca. 1987.

Burckhardt, Titus, *Art of Islam: Language and Meaning,* World of Islam Festival Publishing Company Ltd., Westerham, Kent, England, 1976.

Chebel, Malek, *Symbols of Islam,* Editions Assouline, Paris, 1997.

Clevenot, Domnique, *Splendors of Islam: Architecture, Decoration and Design,* The Vendome Press, NY, 2000.

Husain, Shahrukh, *What do We Know About Islam?,* Peter Burdrick Books, NY, 1995.

Morris, Neil, *Islam: World of Beliefs,* Peter Burdrick Books, Columbus, OH, 2002.

Nardo, Don, *The Persian Empire,* Lucent Books, San Diego, 1998.

Paz, Octavio, *In Praise of Hands,* World Crafts Council, McClelland and Stewart Limited and New York Graphic Society, Greenwich, Ct., 1974.

Tames, Richard, *The Rise of Islam,* Crystal Lake, IL., 1996.

Hands-on Alaska
(ISBN 0-9643177-3-7)

Hands-on America Vol. I
(ISBN 0-9643177-6-1)

Hands-on Rocky Mountains
(ISBN 0-9643177-2-9)

Hands-on Latin America
(ISBN 0-9643177-1-0)

Hands-on Ancient People - Vol. I
(ISBN 0-9643177-8-8)

Hands-on Celebrations
(ISBN 0-9643177-4-5)

Hands-on Pioneers
(ISBN 1-57345-085-5)

Hands-on Africa
(ISBN 0-9643177-7-X)

Hands-on Asia
(ISBN 0-9643177-5-3)

KITS PUBLISHING

Consider these books for: *the library • teaching social studies art • ESL programs multicultural programs • museum programs • community youth events • home schooling*

ORDER FORM

SEND TO:_____

ADDRESS:_____

_____

CITY:_____ STATE:_____ ZIP_____

CONTACT NAME: _____ PHONE: _____

PO # _____ FAX _____

Books are $20⁰⁰ each.

Shipping - $2.00 per book
All books shipped media rate unless otherwise requested.

Make checks payable to:
KITS PUBLISHING • 2359 E. Bryan Avenue • Salt Lake City, Utah 84108
1-801-582-2517 fax: (801) 582-2540
e-mail - info@hands-on.com
Kits Publishing Web site: www.hands-on.com

❒ ____ **Hands-on Africa**

❒ ____ **Hands-on Alaska**

❒ ____ **Hands-on America Vol I**

❒ ____ **Hands-on Ancient People Vol I**

❒ ____ **Hands-on Asia**

❒ ____ **Hands-on Celebrations**

❒ ____ **Hands-on Latin America**

❒ ____ **Hands-on Pioneers**

❒ ____ **Hands-on Rocky Mountains**

_____ Total Quantity Ordered

_3.00_ Handling

_____ Shipping

_____ Total Enclosed/PO